STAY'N *AHEAD* of WHAT'S BEHIND

Jerome G. Silbert

STAY'N AHEAD OF WHAT'S BEHIND

by

Jerome G. Silbert

Stay'n Ahead of What's Behind

Requests for permission should be addressed to:
Jerome G. Silbert
200 S. Wacker Dr. Suite 2650
Chicago, Il 60606
312-207-0181
Jer7979@aol.com

Ebook ISBN: 979-8-9882083-5-6
Paperback ISBN: 979-8-9882083-6-5

Table of Contents

Chapter One

The man wear'n the black robes gazed down upon the defendant from his big-ass chair that sat on a raised platform. The defendant caught the judge sneaking peeks his way.

"Man, I ain't from another planet," he wanted to say but didn't. It made him feel like crap. Although he felt about the same toward the judge. *How can that privileged ass get me? He knows nothin' about me or me, him. We don't travel in the same circles. Ain't that a fact.*

Tired of playing eye tag, the defendant glanced at the bitch sitting next to but below the judge typing every word bein' said. He then focused on the prosecutors who sat at the other table across from him. There were two of them, a good-lookin' ho, long dark hair, and some Irish asshole. Their table was piled with notebooks, photographs, and other shit. They dressed in some fine suits, even the ho.

The defendant's old lady hired some hot-shot mouthpiece. She assured her son the hired lawyer was the best…no need to worry.

The mouthpiece's threads were silky, dark blue with faint reddish pinstripes. The material looked rich and soft as butter. He had a square in his breast pocket and his tie dripped with color. His smile, broad and warm…made one feel at ease. He had told the defendant earlier in the morning it was his lucky suit. *Here's hoping all that shine ain't just show.*

Jasmine, the defendant's woman, gave him some fancy duds, too. Not like the mouthpiece but not disrespectful. It was the first time he wore a white shirt with a button-down collar.

"Ain't sportin' no tie," he warned her. He didn't like things tight around his neck.

The court proceedings didn't unnerve him. It had been a year since the cops busted him. The defendant told everyone it was a frame. Said that to the cops straight up when he got busted, "You gots the wrong homie." The cops called him a name and bent his arms behind his back until it hurt. The police couldn't care less.

The judge said to another of his collection of bitches to call the next case. The clerk leaned over her desk, which was also below the judge's.

"The People v. Lanier, 22 CR 003401," she said.

The defendant perked up. She had called his case.

My mouthpiece stood. Lanier glanced at the vaulted ceiling replicating Michelangelo's painted angels.

* * *

The p-o-l-i-c-e had locked Lanier's ass up after arresting him in his crib. After a while they shoved him into a room, cuffed his wrist to a post and said, "Let's talk." Lanier arched his eyebrows and cursed them under his breath. They told him he had attitude. "Bullshit." Wrong thing to have said.

A Black piece-of-shit, his name, naw they were too smart for that. No name tag. He met Lanier's head with the back of his hand, then said, "Sorry," and did it again, then again. They picked the wrong guy. Lanier bit one of the mothers... They threw his ass back into the cell. G-d knows how long he was there. Couldn't get no sleep, no food, and no place to urinate.

* * *

Lanier's mouthpiece told the court the defense was ready to begin their Motion to Suppress. The judge cleared his throat and looked to the prosecutors. The ho got up and asked to pass the case. He stopped listening. He heard it before.

* * *

Lanier didn't know how much time passed being in that cell. It could have been hours, or days. This older dude, white short-cropped hair, face like a squashed fruit, Garrity or somethin', shouted to someone outside his vision, "He's fine. The prick is staring into space."

What else could Lanier do? There was nothing to lie on. The floor was cement and cold. They treated a dog better. Then this blonde came. She stood outside his cell. She wore a shirt with CPD on it. Didn't catch her name if she said it. Called Lanier like his old lady did... David. Her voice was sweet-like, her hair in a pony, and she smelled fresh. Of course, even in that shit hole his mind, for a second or two, imagined the unimaginable. Lanier was all ears. She told him all he had to do was answer a few questions, then they'd cut him loose.

He nodded.

* * *

The ho sat back down at the prosecutor's table and whispered to the Irish shit. He opened a notebook and pointed at something. Another case was called. The ho stood again this time askin' for a warrant because the mother-fuckin' defendant didn't say, "Here."

Lanier turned to his mouthpiece who stared at his phone.

* * *

Lanier's lawyer, when they were first introduced, had asked his new client if he knew how fish got caught. Lanier replied with a-shit-ass grin, "They open their mouths." Lanier got the point—too late.

The blonde led Lanier into a room. There was another cop, and a lawyer who explained he worked for the State. Well, who didn't, except him. He asked Lanier if he knew his rights like he was in school or something.

Lanier said, "Whatcha mean?" The cop went on reading from a card. When he looked up, he asked if Lanier understood. Lanier wasn't dumb and he understood English. "What about my rights?" Lanier asked.

The cop mumbled something and told him to sign a paper. The blonde was real nice. She let him use the facilities and gave him a cola and a cigarette. Said this was all on tape or somethin'. Lanier looked for the camera but couldn't find it. He scribbled his name on the paper.

Chapter Two

Josiah Pierson Wilson. The brothers called him J.P. He was a product of the south side of Chicago—South Shore neighborhood. Before the late 1960's, the area was considered lace-curtain Irish sprinkled with Jewish folk who didn't know of the northside. That would come later.

J.P. graduated South Shore High School. He was an okay basketball player but got better in his senior year. He avoided the gangs by being smart. He acted as their unofficial consigliere when called upon. His goal was college. His parents, yeah, he had a two-parent household. Pops worked in the steel mills and made a decent living even if he wasn't Irish, German, or Slav. He never missed a day.

Pops was a believer, but a realist. Cutting corners or get-rich schemes never entered his mind. "Hard work, boy, and keep your eyes open for opportunity," was his life's motto. Within the confines of who he was, and the times he traveled, he did all right for himself. He expected J.P. to do better.

Pops wasn't around when J.P. graduated from the fancy full-boat paid law school. He knew of it, though. There were plenty of days sitting at McDonald's with his fellow retirees discussing the issues of the day.

One of Pops' cronies, Henry, on the day of Pops' funeral, told J.P., "Pops managed to throw in a line or two about you, no matter the subject. We'd be discussin' the price of pie at McDonald's. Everyone had an opinion. Price went up cause of inflation. The size shrunk, and out-of-nowhere, Pops puts his coffee down, leans back as if he had something important to say." He imitated Pops' deep voice. "J.P. tells me, the broads in them Ivies are quite something."

Henry placed his hand on J.P.'s shoulder and continued. "The other men, there were three that day, looked at each other, then hid their face in their coffees. They knew what was coming."

Pops in that voice of his began, "J.P. said no matter how rich they are, they … what J.P. call it, 'downplay,' that's what he says. Pretend they're poorer than anyone in Jesus's flock. Can you beat that. Rich people pretending they're poor. What's wrong with this world?"

The other men sipped their coffee and let the story sink in. Then one old geezer, that was Willie McCall, piped up.

"Well, J.P. should fit in good. He don't have to play."

The others roared with laughter.

"What's so funny?" Pops was indignant.

"Drink your coffee," one of them advised. "Whatever J.P. is, he'll be rich soon enough."

* * *

Wealth didn't come so easy, even with a sheepskin from the Ivies. Law firms in Chicago thought him overqualified for the small ones, and he didn't have the connections to the large ones. His choices came down to either join the county state's attorney's or public defender's office, or hang a shingle and go into private practice. His mother told him to pray on it, then meet with the alderman who was friendly to the family.

J.P. opened his office on 71st and Crandon. His mother's friends as well as his drank the punch and Champagne, gorged on the spread, and wished him well. None of that helped with the cash flow. Day in and day out for the first month, he'd stare out his office window wondering if his phone actually worked.

His first client came by way of the alderman. It was a speeding ticket: 90 mph in a 35-mph zone. J.P. obtained the man's record and realized the client was on the verge of losing his license.

J.P. sat back in his Office Depot imitation leather chair, a baby-faced twenty-seven-year-old and solemnly informed his fortyish-looking client of the news.

The client brushed it off. "I needs my car. Can't take no damn bus to get to work. That's why I see the alderman. You're supposed to fix it."

Law schools don't teach the practice of law. Welcome to Chicago.

Chapter Three

The Judge leaned down from his high and mighty place and said someth'n to his bitches while his hand covered the microphone. Lanier couldn't hear. The judge smiled, though. Lanier wondered which one was his squeeze...maybe both. The judge looked past the attorneys' and defendant tables at the people sitting behind the bullet-proof glass shield separatin' the courtroom.

"There will be a ten-minute recess." The judge stood, then walked off the bench.

"What's up? What he need a break for?" Lanier whispered loudly to his attorney.

His mouthpiece, Mr. Wilson, gave him one of them don't-bother-me looks. Wilson glanced at some papers on the table, then turned to Lanier. "What's up with you? You've been here before. If the judge wants to step off the bench, he does it. Maybe he needed to take a piss or call his stockbroker. Jesus, David, relax."

Lanier looked away for a second or two, then saw Mr. Wilson wander over to the prosecutor's table like he on a Sunday stroll. He ignored the asshole Irishman and chatted with the ho. They laughed. Maybe he poundin' her...whatever.

Lanier scratched his ankle. His electronic monitoring device irritated his skin. *Damn that thing. Any little bump and the machine went off and then the sheriff called. Can't do Jasmine properly or anyone else.*

He didn't have much to do while the judge was on break. He turned in his seat and checked out the visitor's gallery. His women folk sat next to each other. He took comfort that they still had his back. It could be worse and have no one like so many of the other dumb shits caught up in the system. He leaned back in his chair. He didn't want to make the bailiff dressed in her oversize sheriff's shirt jumpy. Every time he saw her, that shirt and her big-ass stomach fought to keep all that flesh covered. She probably been in this courtroom a million years and knew all the secrets. A good way to stay in the job along with allowing the alderman or ward boss to pat her ass.

He had lived in Chicago all his twenty-six years. He wasn't blind to how this city worked. Everyone in the building understood, from the janitor to the man who sat on that fancy chair. It was the system. They all, like breathin', knew bread needed to be buttered.

* * *

The court reporter left her chair and went through the door where the judge had gone. Maybe she needed a little excitement to get through the morning. M-a-n, Lanier's imagination was runn'n.

When Lanier was a little chicken hawk in eighth grade and beginn'n high school, he'd get into small crap: "borrowin'" stuff from the neighborhood food store, a few times from the liquor place down the street. No big deal. His hood was changin' and he changed with it. He went from David to his street name, Smilin' Fool or just Fool. He told fantastic stories which led to fists. Didn't matter. It got him to use his head before his mouth.

He was fifteen, nah, fourteen when he busted Pamala Green's cherry. She may have been the last white bitch left in the hood. He told her it was either him or them but sooner or later, and from what he heard on the street, her time was up. He was such a romantic, shit. She wasn't all that good.

Momma on the advice of the alderman and block captain took him to counseling, a joke and a half. Momma didn't like who he was becoming. Didn't like his language. He was fine with it. Matter of fact, the who he was before, and what he was becoming, was all good. He was cool. His homies let him be. Not a member of either the Blackstones or Vice Lords, but he had their respect. He was…eh…what's the word… an independent. His skin color provided access to things the others found difficult to get. Everyone was his friend. The dope and pussy was all a young bull could want. As long as the supply of both kept coming, everyone partied. Everyone was mellow.

Mr. Wilson returned to our table, not saying noth'n but studied his damn phone. The clerk and court reporter took their seats and seconds later the Man, his robe flowing, sat his ass down. He told the clerk to call the case again. My mouthpiece stood along with the ho.

"Are the People ready to proceed?"

"Joclyn Thomas for the People. Your Honor, we learned while you were on break that Detectives Sanchez and Klinaire were on medical leave. I informed Mr. Wilson minutes ago. Neither side can proceed without them."

Wilson nodded. "Correct, your Honor. Both are essential for our Motion to Suppress and quash the arrest. Although, I wish to remind the State as well as this Court these police officers have never appeared despite the many subpoenas that have been issued. This is the fifth time that for one reason or another we cannot move forward."

The Judge gave both sides the eye. "Well…" He stopped, then looked at the ho. "Do you know the nature of their condition?"

She shook her head. Her hair fell over her face. Jesus she was a piece.

"Your Honor, the desk sergeant didn't give us any more information."

"Well, counsel, I'm going to pass the matter one more time. Find out. The Court is losing patience."

Chapter Four

Lanier told his attorney he needed to take a leak. Mr. Wilson shrugged, then warned him to be back in five minutes.

Wilson should know better. Bladders and dicks don't always work when you want them to. *Five minutes...s-h-e-e-t. My body do what my body do.*

Lanier got up and eyed the fat-fuck bailiff. He mouthed bathroom. She nodded.

Jasmine and his momma followed him out the courtroom. He could talk shit to Jasmine but not Momma.

"What's going on, David. I didn't hear all of what the judge said."

He screwed up his face, then sighed. "Same old bullshit. State ain't ready, something like that."

Momma's eyes looked through him.

"I'm tell'n y'all the truth. Honest." He should never have used that word...honest. Momma's eyes flickered as if whatever he said wasn't everything. Couldn't blame her. He'd been a problem for a long time.

* * *

First day of counselling, his blondie social worker asked him about family. Simple question. He told her he was just turnin' thirteen when he went into his garage. There was the old man, feet brushed the roof of the car, hung from the rafters. Can't beat that picture. No sir. The breeze and his weight pushed him forward and back. He swung like he had nothing better to do. He didn't, being dead and all.

Momma screamed when she saw him. Said he had done it to punish her and him. He didn't know if she was mad, scared, or what. She turned around and went into the house. Police came minutes later. The next day's party for him was a funeral instead.

* * *

Jasmine walked with him on his way to the bathroom. He could tell by her eyes she had something else on her mind. Her hands clawed his back. At that moment she would have liked him usin' his thing for something other than peeing. "We'll get down to business real soon," he said and grabbed her hand. "This court crap is goin' be continued again."

She frowned. "I don't like bein' at your momma's house. I can't let go knowin' momma outside the bedroom door."

He pulled Jasmine closer. "It ain't like my old lady hadn't heard it before." He gave Jasmine tongue, then smacked her ass. "We'll party later tonight, I promise," he told her and left her at the bathroom door.

Steppin' back into the courtroom, he saw Mr. Wilson eye him and point to his watch. *Fuck him,* he thought, but said, "Sorry, nothin' workin' like it should." He gave a quick peek at the ho. Couldn't see Wilson's expression, but Lanier noticed hers. Wilson must have her lined up after this shit was over. *He gots his and I gots mine.* But you know the eye was never satisfied.

The clerk called his name. She had his attention. My mouthpiece stood. So did the ho. They shot the breeze at each other. I lost interest until the judge said, "Enough." He looked pissed and told the ho to get the State's act together or there would be a come-uppance. Lanier tried not to smile. The judge said that the last time.

Mr. Wilson asked if the new date was all right. It was two months from now. "Sure, but can you ask the judge to get this shit off my leg?"

Wilson shushed him, then told the judge the date was agreed.

Lanier followed his mouthpiece out the courtroom and stood by Jasmine. The mouthpiece and Momma went over by a side corridor. Momma must have slipped him some green. Those nice suits he wore cost. Their business done, they walked toward Lanier. Momma wasn't smilin'. The Mouthpiece covered the distance quickly. He took in Jasmine. He may be a mouthpiece, but he was a dog like any other brother. He was smooth, though. Only his eyes strayed for a second or two, then he turned his attention to Lanier.

"David, I need you to come to the office in a few weeks. The Judge is coming down hard on the State and I think our Motion is going to go the next time we're here."

Lanier took a half-step back as if he'd been slapped. He didn't like being called by his real name. He saw Jasmine out of the corner of his eye smirk. Nothin' he could do about it. That's what his momma and papa named him. D-a-v-i-d, big-time king of Israel. The Bible described him as a lady's man. Fucked any woman in sight. Tricked up his best friend to get Bathsheba, then rapped about it. His shit was still playing. With that kind of history, he'd live with it.

He nodded. Mr. Wilson told him the last time to be ready. Wilson was lookin' straight at him, waitin' for something more. He stared back. Certainly, he wasn't going to talk in front of Jasmine. He wasn't stupid. He grabbed his woman around the waist. "Gots to go, Mr. Wilson. I'll catch you up. Jasmine has the wheels."

Chapter Five

J.P. watched as David, Jasmine, and Mrs. Lanier walked toward the bank of elevators down the hallway. Even after practicing law for twenty years, he didn't understand the nonchalance of defendants facing time in prison. He would be a mess if it was the other way around. His phone purred. He had another case in another courtroom, and the parties were waiting.

Back when he was starting out, J.P. did what any newbie lawyer did. He took whoever walked into his neighborhood office door, no matter the case. He didn't drive a big ol' Lincoln or Caddy, and his clothes had tags from Marshalls. It wasn't glamorous like *Suits*.

Clients. He needed them but soon learned not all were worth having. There were some who looked him in the eye, swore on their mother they were telling the G-d's honest truth only for him to discover they were selling garbage.

An older lawyer sat him down one day in the basement of the Chicago Daley Center. They ordered coffee, then grabbed one of the tables. It had been a bad day. J.P. beat a driving under the influence case. As soon as the judge uttered "Not Guilty," the client made a fast exit out the door along with J.P.'s fee.

The older man, the fluorescent lights dancing off his almost bald head, took a sip, then poured several packets of sugar into his cup. He smiled. "I don't say this to almost anyone, but J.P., you have a future. I know you do. You've got presence and smarts."

"If I'm all that good, why did that asshole stiff me? Why didn't I see it?"

"Clients are no better or worse than anyone else. Some look at you to further their con they already in. Others see you as the magic man. They watch too much TV. They think that license hang'n on your wall entitles them to a 'get-out-of-jail-free' card. Then there are those who play you. They want to take not just your skill, but your soul and pay you nothin' for it. Those are the ones you need to watch out for. They'll ruin you, emotionally and financially.

"You the lawyer, act the part. People pay for what they see. No matter if they're cryin' and tell you they have nothing. Get the money up front, or as much as you can. You're still doin' God's work, but you're getting paid for it."

It took a few years, but J.P. got the message. He teamed up with two others: Elijah Jones and Daniel Singer. J.P.'s mother beamed when she saw the engraved sign of Wilson, Jones, and Singer outside of their downtown office suite. His suits weren't custom but off the rack from Nordstrom's. He drove a red Mazda two-seater, license plate GAMEOVER.

After several years with Jones and Singer, J.P. decided it was high time to be on his own again. He was forty-five. This time, being solo wasn't the same. He had a staff and a fancy office on the 35th floor of 221 N. La Salle in Chicago. The gold lettering on the outside of the front door read **J.P. Wilson & Associates.**

* * *

J.P. stepped toward the bench with his other client. A violation of probation matter that took a few minutes to argue for a continuance. The judge agreed and ordered a new date. J.P. walked his client out the door. "I persuaded the judge to give you one more chance to pay your fine and finish your community service. Don't piss him off."

The man nodded. "Don't you worry, Mr. Wilson. I'll get it done. You can be sure of it." The man reached into his pocket and subtly handed J.P. more green. "That's five bills. I'll have more next time."

"Make sure on both accounts."

The client turned away and headed toward the elevators.

J.P. pocketed the cash and was about to check his phone but noticed a text message. "Lunch?" He smiled and took a deep breath.

* * *

The waiting area in J.P.'s new office had rich wood panels and a large Persian rug on the floor. Expensive modern paintings hung on the walls with soft lighting accentuating them.

His office windows caught the Chicago River and the skyscrapers that touched the river walk. His chairs were made of rich soft leather.

J.P.'s suits were now made by Enzo, the Mazda replaced by a Lexus LC. The license plate stayed the same.

The opening of J.P.'s new offices was filled with other attorneys, judges, government officials, and friends. There was no one from the old neighborhood and his mother didn't live to see it.

Looking at the happy throng, J.P. remembered that old lawyer who sat him down at the Daley Center. Image was everything. A potential client had only to scan the walls and take in the furnishing. *We're talking money. We're talking... success.*

Chapter Six

Fool didn't live in the ghetto. At least it wasn't at the time his family moved there. Then again, the whole south side of Chicago was one big turf, if you got his drift.

Jasmine eased the ride down South Shore Drive, past Hyde Park, then Jackson Park. Obama's big deal ain't too far. Construction everywhere makin' traffic slow. My woman had one hand on the wheel and the other on my crotch. Pullin' on my zipper.

"Cut that out. We both know it works and works fine."

"I ain't doin' nothin'." She jerked her hand away and laid on the gas. The car jumped.

"You tryin' to get us killed? I don't need no more trouble. Slow down. Momma's goin' shoppin' and then grabbin' some joe with a girlfriend. We got plenty of time."

She gave him one of them icy looks. Her eyes let him know what was comin'.

"Maybe I don't want what you got in them pants no more. I'm tired of your place. Goin' nowhere, no movies, clubbin', or dancin'. I don't wants to be no wife to you. I'm young. We partied every night before you got yourself locked up. You were fun. Now…" Her voice trailed off.

He heard the bitchin' before. Jasmine puts out and she puts out good, but lordy, there was always a price. She wasn't no ho. Didn't mean it that way. But there ain't no somethin' for nothin'.

"Hey. The mouthpiece said the case was goin' next time. He seemed to mean it. Two months, baby, that's all it'll take. You'll be steppin' out in fine new shoes and clothes," he promised.

Jasmine put both hands on the wheel. She gave him a quick glance, then turned back to the road.

"You think I like being cooped up in Momma's crib and not have one of my own? I'm a grown man. The Man makes me stay at Momma's. Thanks to this piece of shit attached to my leg."

They stopped at a light on 67th and Jeffery. He saw little lines creep across her forehead. The girl was thinkin'. "I need to eat if jump'n bones still on your mind," she said. "Let's go to Q and Jerk over by Yates."

He checked the time on his watch. The sheriff only gave him forty-five minutes to get from the courthouse back to Momma's. It'd be tight. He checked out Jasmine. What the hell. Bad traffic, he'd say, if the Man called.

They drove into the lot. "Girl, get us a whole platter of that jerk chicken. Here's a twenty-spot."

She grabbed the cash and got out of the car. She knew he was lookin' at her as she walked into the place. She was right. She was as fine a piece as you can get. The Lord blessed her with a pretty face, tits, and one hell of an ass. She disappeared into the joint. He waited. Five minutes passed, then ten. His watch didn't lie. He scanned the parking lot. There wasn't many cars. What was goin' on? Another five went by. This ain't right. He stepped out and took a few steps toward the front door. Two homies came out. One was about six feet, the other shorter. They flashed their gang signs…BD, Black Disciples. He recognized most of the signs and flashed back. The tall dude shook his head. A sick smile crossed his face.

"You ain't no BD, asshole." His hands rested near his belt.

Lanier didn't blink or show fear. "Yo, I knows that. I gets a pass."

Both of them laughed. "Listen, Fool, your magic is gone. You ain't shit no more. It's a changed scene. Get back into that whip of yours."

"I'm waitin' for my woman."

They took a quick peek into the joint. They laughed. "Umm, she kind of busy."

He shuffled his feet. "Whatcha mean? She's gettin' some chicken."

The tall dude flashed his piece. "Don't come no further, bro. She's gett'n some but it ain't no chicken."

"Jasmine, get your ass over here," he shouted.

"Shoot the mother," the shorter dude said.

He stared at the two assholes. "Don't want no trouble. I'll take my woman and go."

"Shoot him. He got a piece in the whip."

He threw his hands up. "You crazy. I'm already in deep shit."

The tall one lowered his Glock a bit. "I'm givin' you advice. You ain't welcome no more. Get your skinny white ass out of the hood. You ain't one of us. You never was. Leave the ride and your bitch and start walkin'. We see you on the street or in your Momma's crib, we ain't goin' to be so nice."

"I still say shoot the fucker." The little dude was hoppin' up and down.

He heard the other one say, "Too many eyes. Get in and get yourself a piece while there's still somethin' to get. Don't know how long she'll last."

The little shit went inside. Lanier took the dude's advice.

Chapter Seven

Mrs. Anne Lanier had parked her car at the 26th Street courthouse parking garage. Although she would be breathless upon reaching the third floor, the garbage-laden steps were better than to be stuck in the metal container that posed as an elevator of some sort. Everything about the lot as well as the courthouse was old and tired…too much misery in one place.

David had told her that behind the stone courthouse was the Cook County Jail. A barbed wire fence encircled the edifice. Chicago cops, County cops, other police from other jurisdictions were all over the complex. More firepower than a small army. All to keep a few thousand souls in and everybody else out.

Anne started her car and drove down several ramps until she cleared the parking garage. Before turning onto the boulevard, she faced the squat, grey stone courthouse. Society's answer to kindergarten children who continued to misbehave; only the punishment changed from standing in the corner to a jail cell.

She shuddered each time she saw it. There was no humanness in its structure, inside or out.

She feared what could happen to her son, David. The penitentiary was a real possibility—a waste of human life. David, with all his potential, thrown away like garbage. He had been an "A" student until…it no longer mattered…what could have been. She had to deal with the reality of what is.

She had told David many times, the people he hung with were not friends. *You lie with dogs; you wake up with fleas.* She never won the arguments.

She should have moved out of the neighborhood while there was a chance. She should of… She gripped her steering wheel harder. It was too late to correct her mistake. She wanted to prove a point. She wanted to be an example to not only talk the talk but walk the walk to her liberal friends and herself. She stayed. The neighborhood changed, and so too, her son.

Anne's girlfriend, whom she was meeting in Hyde Park, would have told her she was full of shit. David had his own mind. He knew right from wrong. It wasn't the neighborhood.

Easy for Charise. It's hard to watch one's only son reject everything you've given him. He must have known on some level he was going down the devil's path. Then again, she should have forcibly stepped in. Taken a firmer hand. But she had her own issues. A husband that killed himself. The shame of it all. It immobilized her. She wasn't even there for herself, much less for David.

She weighed canceling her coffee date with Charise. The court appearances spread over a year had taken its toll. Socializing was not high on her list. She hit the little button to call her friend, then thought otherwise. What was she coming home to? David and that cheap bitch, Jasmine, doing it wherever they pleased. There was no good future for them. Eventually, Jasmine would get pregnant. Then what? She tried to hold back the tears, but her eyes didn't obey. She grabbed Kleenex out of her purse to stem her cry.

The exit for Hyde Park was coming up on her right. She checked the mirrors to move over, when her car speaker announced she was receiving a phone call. The screen read "JASMINE". What the hell? She had never called Anne. *David. Something happened to him.* Her finger hovered over the Answer button. She could feel her heart quicken, and her mouth became dry as she braced herself.

"Hello," Anne said.

"Momma Anne..." Jasmine's voice quivered choked with tears. "Awful...he...they..."

"I can't understand you. What happened? Where are you?"

"Momma...Anne...come...get...me. Please...come...get..."

"Where's David?" Anne heard static and asked again.

"Q and Jerk...a block..."

"Jasmine?" Anne knew what a gunshot sounded like, and she was sure that's what she heard. "Jasmine? Hello?" She heard laughter in response, then a male voice, "bitch".

Chapter Eight

Fool took two buses and made it home. As he unlocked the door, he heard the phone's relentless toll. He was late...way late. His electronic monitor danc'n up a storm. The Law gettin' ready to snatch him away with each unanswered ring.

"Mama, get the phone, damn it. It's the County." She didn't answer. He raced to the kitchen and grabbed the yellow receiver off the wall.

"Hello, hello." Too late, there was no one on the other end. He gazed at the ceiling as if he never saw the cracks and chipped paint before. The place was a sty—falling apart like everything else in his life. What to do? The County will be at his crib soon enough. The BD's will kill him in jail—not an option. Stay'n'—not an option, either.

He raced down the stairs to the basement and found a hammer lying on a shelf with other tools. It took three swings to get the motherfuck'n electronic device off his ankle. No time to look at his work. He ran back up and barged into his mother's room. Momma always had a stash. He went straight to the shoe box in her closet. Threw the shoes to the floor and grabbed all of it. He saw a Franklin on top and stuffed the bills in his pocket. He'd count the rest later.

In his room, he grabbed a backpack from his school days and filled it with underwear, socks, two shirts, a pair of jeans, and a hoodie.

He glanced around his room after throwing the last piece of clothing into the bag. The aged posters of Michael Jordan and the other MJ still hung on the wall. Jasmine never liked staring at them while they were getting it on.

Jasmine. Did the bitch betray him or did the gang fuck her up as a warning. No matter now. He didn't have time to get sentimental.

He stepped into the hallway and listened. Hearing nothing, he went to the front of the house and peeked out the front window. The street appeared quiet. He then went to the back. He lowered his baseball cap, then raised his jacket collar. *Hope to G-d no one sees.* He dumped his phone in the garbage and snuck out the door.

* * *

Anne redialed Jasmine after the call was cut off. She barely noticed the hum the line made to reconnect. Her words spilled out. "Jasmine, where are you? Tell me...please. Are you..." No voice answered, only the buzz in search of the connection. She pushed the End button. She imagined the worst...Jasmine was shot...murdered? *Oh, my G-d. David! Was David killed too?* She couldn't continue to drive and have those thoughts swirling in her head. She pulled over. *I have to call David.* In a shaky voice, she commanded the car system to make the call. David didn't answer. Her hand covered her mouth. A wave of nausea washed over her. *Am I having a heart attack*, she thought? She opened the window and leaned out. The cold air struck her face. The urge subsided and she caught her breath. Her hands were cold and her whole body trembled. *Have to get a hold of myself. I can't fall apart.* She closed the window and sat. For several seconds or minutes, she stared out the window not seeing anything. Then her phone rang. She jumped, her head scraping the car's ceiling. "Hello," she yelled.

"Anne?" a female voice asked.

The voice disoriented Anne. It took a beat or two until she recognized it. It was Charise, her coffee date.

"Char—" Anne began and burst into tears.

"What's wrong?"

"I... I...it's too horrible..."

"Where are you?"

Anne wiped her eyes with her sleeve and looked out the window. "I'm on—on the Drive?" She blinked and searched for a sign... or a landmark. "I...near...Forty-seventh Street exit, I think." She looked over her shoulder for anything recognizable.

"I'm hunting for parking near Café 53 on Fifty-third St. Can you get yourself over here?"

Anne took a deep breath. She squeezed her hands to stop their trembling and stimulate circulation. "Yeah...sure..." There was a long pause. "Just got to get it together. Thank you, Char. You called in the nick of time...I don't know..." Her voice trailed off.

"It's okay. Whatever it is, it'll be all right."

"Don't say that, Charise. You don't know."

"Comme on, Anne, after what you've been—"
"I think Jasmine is dead and maybe David."
"What?… Holy shit."

Chapter Nine

J.P. stood in the hallway on the seventh floor of the courthouse. He checked the time. Lunch. The days when that would be a lonely affair were long gone. Now... everyone wanted to break bread with him. He responded to the invitation received while in court with a yes and suggested an old Chicago favorite, Manny's, a cafeteria-style deli. It catered to all: politicians of every stripe, cops, firemen, lawyers, you name it, they were there chowing down on the corned beef and potato pancakes. Jews knew how to run a deli. The response came with a smiley face.

He strode through the courthouse halls, nodded to the greetings of fellow attorneys, cracking a one-liner here and there. He was stopped several times by defendants or their relatives beseeching him for his card. It was an everyday occurrence, like a king reviewing the troops. He was the miracle worker. The man who could set them free. No more traffic tickets unless it was a celebrity or politician who screwed up. The publicity then was golden, as well as the fee.

He pushed the revolving doors and stepped outside to head for the parking lot. The wind made its presence known. It may have been a half a block walk, but the bluster of its frigid air made one move quickly. If this was Wrigley Field, there would have been home runs galore.

His Lexus LX500s was parked on the first floor in a spot unofficially reserved for him. Anyone who frequented the courthouse knew the spot was his.

He did a cursory inspection of his vehicle, then unlocked the car by touching the door handle. No need for keys or pressing fobs to open it. He dropped his briefcase on the passenger seat and allowed the driver's plush leather seat to envelop him. He took a moment to exhale and leave some of the pressure behind. He scanned the phone that was in his hand and caught a glimpse of the smiley face response that remained on the screen. Lunch with Nora James. She was the receptionist to Joclyn Thomas's boss. A delightful thirtyish woman who had wit and a figure to match. She also had information that she doled out judiciously.

It took about twenty minutes to get to Manny's and another five to find an available space in their lot. He spotted Nora's car already parked and wondered how she beat him. He rounded the corner from the parking lot and saw her standing in front of the restaurant.

"What took?" she asked.

"I was going to ask you the same thing."

"Huh, I've been here waiting…" her eyes smiling.

"How long?"

She shrugged. "Can't lie. Just got here. The light at the corner must have held you up."

"I suppose…anyway, nice to see you. Hungry?"

"You betcha. I love this place."

* * *

Joclyn Thomas, along with her trial partner Bob O'Dell, left their courtroom. O'Dell pushed their cart full of that day's files and waited for the elevator.

"Lunch?" he asked.

"What did you have in mind? I brought a sandwich. Didn't think we'd have time, but…" Her eyes glazed upward. She paused, then asked, "What do you think is really going on with those cops on Lanier's case?"

O'Dell put his index finger to his lips. His eyes swept the several people, also waiting.

She followed his gaze. "Got it. Let's…uhm…I have a taste for Italian. How about you?"

"Too heavy." He patted his stomach. "It's growing like a mother… Let's stay in the building."

"You've got to be… I'll eat my sandwich. The hell with it and I'll save money to boot."

The ancient elevator came, and they squeezed their way in. The car was large and already filled with cops, defendants, and G-d knows who else. The metal door slowly clanged shut. It was a relief when they made it to the first floor.

26th & Cal was a busy place. A block-long corridor connected the courthouse to the office building where they were going. Another bank of elevators took them to their offices on the eleventh floor.

O'Dell pushed the cart out of the car with Joclyn following behind. Another receptionist, Alice, looked up. "Stop. Hold on there. I have a call for you, Ms. Thomas. Lt. Brainer from the Sheriff's department is on the line for you. I'll put it through to your office."

"Thanks." She quickened her pace, all the while wondering who the hell was Lt. Brainer and what did he want. High heels weren't the ideal running shoes, but she reached her office just as her phone began to ring. She caught her breath, then answered. "Assistant State's Attorney Thomas."

"Hello. I'm Lt. Brainer in charge of the electronic monitoring program. One of your defendants, a David Lanier, is missing."

"Missing? What do you mean?"

"We tracked him leaving court. After the allotted time he was given, we called his home. There was no answer. Then the signal went dead."

"Shit. Did you contact his attorney?"

"No. That's up to you."

"Okay. Thanks for the update. Are you filing for an arrest warrant?"

"That's why I called."

"You got it. I'll prepare it right away. Email all the info."

"Will do. Thanks, Ms. Thomas."

Joclyn hung up the phone. So much for lunch.

Chapter Ten

There were three things Fool figured he needed to do while being on the run. He ticked them off, but they all added up to one: keep out-of-sight. Hell, he watched enough TV shows and movies. Staying low meant staying alive and that was a great motivator. It was the "how" that was difficult.

First things first, he had to get out of the hood. A white guy in a Black area was like a Black dude in one of them rich northern suburbs. They stuck out. He thought of Jasmine's place, but that notion was out of the question. She was either raped or from what he could tell, switched sides. Either way it was a bust; besides, the cops would be waiting for him. Feeling sorry for himself or her would come later. Going north toward Hyde Park and downtown was a possibility. The other was southeast to Indiana. The distance was about the same, but Hammond had casinos and crowds, and most importantly, it was very much out of Cook County, Illinois. A good place to get lost and maybe make some green.

He stuck to the alleys and shadows and pulled his hat down as far as it could go. He zigzagged until he reached 95th and Stony Island. The street always had a lot of truck traffic, much of it heading to Indiana. He had to take a chance. He stuck his thumb out and ten minutes later a white Ford van stopped.

"Where you headn'?" asked a 40ish looking woman.

"Hammond."

"Get in. Go'n there myself. Got loose change in my pocket, so to speak."

He closed the door and felt the dice rolling his way. "Go there often?"

"Often enough." She hit the accelerator, and they were on their way.

"Which casino you find lucky?"

She gave him a once-over. "You a virgin or something? Never been to one, eh?"

"Hey..." He felt his cheeks flush. "Hell..." He shrugged. "No, ma'am."

She let out a laugh. "Got me a virgin." She eyed him again. "And a good-look'n stud. You got a roll?"

"A what?"

"Money, greenhorn. You need scratch if you're going to gamble."

He hesitated. He moved his hand from his lap and rested it on the side of his pants leg where he felt the outline of his stolen booty. "Yeah, I gots some."

"Some?"

"Enough to see me through."

She laughed. "We'll see."

* * *

J.P. and Nora stood in line at Manny's cafeteria. A crowd of people were in front of them, all waiting to be served.

"Every time I'm here, I think of the corned beef but then I'm standing in this queue and see all these other choices: salads, chicken, potato knishes. What's a girl to do?" Nora asked.

J.P. smiled. "You mean there's something other than a sandwich stacked to the ceiling on rye with hot mustard?"

"Jesus, you make a convincing argument, counselor."

"Thought so."

J.P. paid the tab for their lunches and found two seats at a table. After they sat, he reached for a dill pickle on his plate. He caught Nora, who sat across from him, biting into her treasure. Her eyes danced with glee as she swallowed a small portion.

"G-d...what was I thinking. 'Heaven'," she pointed to her sandwich, "J.P.... heaven."

"You sure love what you love."

"That's my rep—no middle ground for me."

"Hmm. Is that for food or everything else in your life?"

"Very funny. What do you think?"

"I say, it's time to sample what's in front of me." He smiled. "Then have a cigarette."

He gripped half of his sandwich with both hands and bit in. Before he could say anything, Nora quipped, "Was it as good for you as it was for me?"

He nodded. "Better."

A look of surprise came over her. "Couldn't be," and took another bite. She pointed again to her food, "it's a good thing I don't come here on a regular basis." She took a sip of her cola. "Soooo… Have you made the world a little more unsafe today by convincing judges to let your guilty clients go free?"

"Now, Nora, I only represent innocent people." He waited a few seconds. "That's what they all tell me."

"Uh-huh. How's that Lanier case going with my best bud Joclyn?"

J.P. ate more of his sandwich and savored the taste. "You know what the secret to this food is?"

"What?"

"Schmaltz. It's Yiddish for fat. If the corned beef doesn't have a little bit of schmaltz, it's like eating paper."

"Yeah, well whatever, it's delicious and I know not good for you."

"You can bet on that." He picked up a fallen shred of corned beef. "What do you know about Detectives Sanchez and Klinaire out of Central district?"

"What makes you think I know anything?" Her eyes gave her hidden smile away. She stuffed a piece of potato pancake in her mouth. After she swallowed, she asked, "I suppose that too has smaltze… or whatever you called it.

He shook his head.

"They're on bad…"

His cell phone buzzed. "Hold on, I have to take this."

"Sure."

J.P. answered. His secretary related her conversation with ASA Joclyn Thomas. David Lanier was on the run. "Damn," he said. "Stupid, stupid," and hung up.

"Bad news?" Nora asked.

"Looks like it." He pushed his plate, with a half sandwich left, away.

"Really? That lousy?"

"If you want it, it's all yours. Sorry to do this but I have to run." He stood. "You were about to say those dicks were on bad paper?"

"Huh?" She looked at him after grabbing his corned beef on rye. "Yeah, some sort of investigation. Hush, hush."

"Thanks, Nora. Enjoy the lunch. Hell, maybe we can work this into a dinner."

"Lunch interruptus leads to a…? Go. We'll talk later."

He left, rushing to his car, savoring her comment and worried about his client.

Chapter Eleven

It took more time than usual for Anne to drive to Café 53. Her attention wasn't on her speed, but on the radio tuned to WBBM. She hoped there would be a news story about her son or Jasmine. The announcer blabbed on about the sports, weather, and traffic, and someone gave her the finger for driving too slowly.

Her world was again spiraling out of control, like when she found her husband dangling from the ceiling. She thought she was through with that memory, but Jasmine's call brought it back. The rawness and crushing weight hit her. What if she lost David? Her husband left her a widow but if her son died... Oh G-d, she couldn't come to grips with that. Her only child...gone...so young...before he had a chance in this world. She kept herself from going hysterical by chanting, "I'll be okay," and almost missed the vacant spot a few doors down from the Café. It was a crappy parking job but so be it. Her knees felt weak. She grabbed the car door frame to get out. Her friend Charise rushed over to help.

"I was by the entrance and saw you. I gotcha, girl. We'll sort all this out. Use my arm for support."

Anne took a breath, then stood straight. "I'm okay. Really. I'm not that gone that I can't do this myself." She took two steps, stumbled slightly, but waved Charise off. "Let's get a table. I can use a large coffee...as big as they have."

"No problem."

They found a spot near the back but with a good view of the 60" TV monitor set into the modern décor wall space.

"What do you want in it?" Charise asked while Anne surrendered herself to her chair.

"Huh?"

"Your coffee, remember?"

"Oh yeah." A tight smile crossed her lips. "Nothing, nothing at all, straight black."

Charise nodded. "I thought so," and headed toward the bar.

It took several minutes, longer than Anne wished. She needed coffee or something to pierce her descending fog. She kept an eye on the TV as well as on her friend. She could tell the barista and Charise were engaged in banter. Instead of the laughter she heard, she envisioned smacking them both while demanding her order to be filled. She was working herself into a very bad place. Finally, Charise walked back with their drinks.

"Oooh, that barista sure is—"

Anne shot out of her chair and stared at the TV. In the background of the picture was the parking lot of Q and Jerk. The reporter on the scene said something about the police investigating…

"What? What are they investigating?" Anne shouted.

Coffee splattered on the table as Anne resumed her seat. "Charise, did you catch…"

She shook her head. "Sorry, I…" She dropped several napkins over the spill. "Drink, Anne, catch your breath. Then tell me what's going on."

* * *

"As soon as I get on the Ford freeway we'll be going through the armpit of Chicago." The driver of the van glanced at her passenger. "I'm Sonny, by the way. My folks named me Gretchen, but Sonny is more to my liking. What's yours?"

"David," and after a slight hesitation, "Fool, Smile'n Fool or just Fool."

"Interesting…any particular reason?"

He shrugged. "Guess I smile a lot and do stupid things."

"Good to know, well Dav, eh, Fool, roll up that window. It stinks out here. Hate going through these parts. The smells of the old steel mills and factories' pollution are still here. Worse years ago, but still bad."

Fool let what passed as scenery roll by. "It shouldn't be too long before we're in Hammond?"

"Right, you are but…look at this damn traffic." She flicked on the radio. "Let's hear how bad."

Fool stared out the front window and saw trucks. Big ones, small ones, mixed in with regular people in cars heading east. All three lanes jammed. "Don't need a report to tell it's a shit ride to Hammond." He grabbed the tuner dial and was about to move it.

"And what in G-d's name do you think you're doing?"

"Huh?" He must have had the look of a child with his hand caught in the cookie jar.

"Don't you dare touch my radio. My car, Fool. If you don't like it, I'll let you out here. You can walk."

"Okay, okay. Just thought music would be better to pass the time. They ain't go'n to say anything different than what you see."

She stared out the driver's window, seemingly thinking over what he said. After a minute or two of commercials, she must have lost patience. "What station you like?"

He shrugged. "Makes no difference as long as it's music."

"No difference, eh? Opera?" She laughed. "Beethoven, the Boss, rap? What's it going to be?"

"Rock and roll..." He paused. "Beethoven was a badass dude. He did all right with his music. Nine symphonies, most of them made up while his hearing was going. Sweet."

Her jaw dropped a bit. "You know from...the hell with it. Rock and roll it is."

It took about an hour before Sonny rolled up the driveway of the Hard Rock casino. "Okay, Fool. End of the ride."

"Huh? You ain't go'n in here?"

She gave him a long hard look. "Kid, you're nice enough but you could cramp my ways. I don't need a hunk around when I'm also look'n for one. Besides there are younger treats than someone like me. You get it, Fool? This ain't only a place to gamble—" Her eyes widened. "All sorts of enticements to gamble on."

"Wasn't think'n about that other stuff. No problem." He glanced at the large neon sign above the door. "*Hard Rock.* Didn't know they casinos. Thought it was a café or someth'n." He opened the door and stepped out. "Hope Lady Luck got your back. Thanks for the ride, Sonny."

She pulled away and waved.

Chapter Twelve

J.P. gave his Lexus to Julio, the twenty-something parking attendant in his building.

"Nice wheels, Mr. Wilson." Julio whistled as he popped into the driver's seat. "Must cost a few pesos."

"You got that right. Be careful with it."

"Yes sir."

Julio went speeding up the ramp, causing the tires to squeal as he made a sharp turn. J.P. jerked his head in that direction, but the car disappeared. He waited a few seconds more, shook his head, then went out of the garage and into the building. He checked his phone as he walked to the elevator, hunting for an update on Lanier. Not seeing any, he switched to the *Sun-Times* app. His search was interrupted by the elevator's arrival. It took several seconds to whisk him to the 35th floor and his office. He still had his cell in his hand when he entered.

He walked through the seating area while taking notice no one was waiting. "Anything more on Lanier?"

Tasha, his secretary, replied, "No, but I have Ms. Thomas's number if you'd want to reach her."

He took the message paper from her and went to his office, closing the door. What he should do was try to reach Lanier first, and if he couldn't, call Lanier's mother. He sat at his desk and dialed his client from his landline. The call went immediately to voice mail. *Shit.* He then went through his file for the mother's number. A quick search found it. He punched in the numerals. On the third ring, the call connected.

"Hello?"

"Anne, this is J.P.... Mr. Wilson. I've been trying to reach your son. Do you know where he is?"

"No." Her voice caught. "I—got a call... from Jasmine..."

He heard her breathe heavily into the phone.

"She needed...help. I heard a gun...Oh my G-d, what if...David...what...David."

"Anne, please. I know this is difficult..." He moved the receiver from his ear as her crying filled the air. He heard another female voice talking to Anne.

"Where are you?" he asked.

"Mr. Wilson, I'm Anne's friend, Charise. We're at Café 53 in Hyde Park. As you can tell, Anne is terribly upset. She got a phone call from David's girlfriend, Jasmine. She told Anne she needed help and that she was at the Q and Jerk. Anne then heard a gunshot, and the call went dead. Anne and I have been scouring the news but haven't found anything more."

"Give me that information again. Q and...?"

"Jerk, around Seventy-first and Yates."

J.P. could picture the area but not the restaurant. *Must have got there after I moved.* "Thank you, Char—"

"—ise, Charise. What do we do, Mr. Wilson?"

J.P. swiveled in his chair so that he could peek at the lake. He hated the drama that a client dumps on their family. They suffer as much if not more than the defendant. They're the spectators in a play not their making. He had taken notes, and he quickly reviewed what he had scribbled. "What time did Anne get this call from Jasmine?" He turned toward his desk.

"What time did you get that call, Anne?" Charise asked.

"I don't... give me my phone. I'll check it."

J.P. waited several seconds, listening to Anne and Charise.

"Hello, Mr. Wilson?"

"Yes...Anne I'm here."

"I got the call about 1:30. Can you do something?"

J.P. dropped his pen on his yellow pad. "I'll make some calls. If David phones, get a hold of me right away. There's a warrant for his arrest. I'll contact you later today."

"Thank you, Mr. Wilson. Please let me know if you find something...anything." Anne paused. "Do you think I should go there?"

"Where?"

"The Q and Jerk."

"No, definitely don't do that. Do you have any idea where David could be?"

"Could be? Mr. Wilson I'm praying he's somewhere still on this earth."

* * *

Jasmine gave the phone back to the dude known as Big Hit. "Did you have to fire that rod so close to me? My ears still ringin'."

"So's your pussy from all that action. Get into the fuck'n car."

They were outside the Q and Jerk. The three dudes left the restaurant after they had fucked Jasmine. They gave a high sign to Big Hit and smiled. The little dude who had been with Big Hit confronting Fool walked out the door straightening his pants behind the other three.

Jasmine stood outside Big Hit's ride combed her hair, then buttoned her blouse and jeans.

"Get your ass in there."

"My booty moves when I want it to move."

Big Hit took a step toward her.

"All right I'm go'n but that small fry better not be comin' along. Of all the dudes he be the nastiest as well as packing an attitude. He twisted my tits like a bottle cap. What's wrong with him. Hasn't he fucked a woman before?"

Big Hit grabbed Jasmine by the back of her neck, opened the passenger door of his Cadillac SUV, and flung her in like a rag doll. "Shut up. We gots to move." He climbed into the driver's seat and waited for Short Stuff to jump in on the front passenger side. He then toggled the automatic locks button.

Jasmine righted herself and dug her hands into the seat. "Shit are you going to do me now. Like bang, I'm dead?"

"Girl, you got initiated," Big Hit said, stepping on the gas and tearing out of the parking lot. "You with us now. That white piece of shit, Fool, no longer your life. His momma thinks you dead. The front man at the Q will tell the pigs all the right things." He made a right turn and hopped on South Shore Dr. "You put on a real nice show. Dat's good. You do right with us, and you'll have all the clothes, dope, and dicks you want. You'll be the reward to those who deserve such a fine piece."

"Hmm. You know, Big," she sat back in the seat, "if I be the prize, I should have some say. That way there'd be like competition. What happened now was like a dream. Being with Fool and his dumb-ass momma was a prison. Don't want to go back."

"Glad we have an understand'n," Big said, giving Short Stuff a wink.

Short Stuff turned in his seat toward Jasmine. "Dat's right." He snatched at her leg, but she moved to the other side. "Come here, bitch."

"Don't let him talk to me like that." She grabbed the back of Big Hit's seat. "That's what I'm say'n. I choose who I put out for. Got it? That boy messed me up." She rubbed her chest.

Big Hit did a quick glance toward her. His neck muscles bulged. "You don't make the rules. You do what I say. There ain't more to discuss."

Jasmine sat back, stuck her jaw out, and stared at Short Stuff. She put her hands between her legs and mouthed, "nothin' for you."

Chapter Thirteen

Fool shoved his hand into his pants pocket. The feel of the green gave him confidence. He go'n to clean up. All those dice games and nighttime poker he played between shots, dope, and bitches prepared him for this. He checked out the huge sign above the entrance. *This ain't noth'n.* He stepped through the casino door.

"Welcome to Hard Rock," said a bitch with long blonde hair, wearing a tight black dress.

Fool jerked his head in acknowledgement.

"First time?"

"What?" He stared at her not sure of her meaning. Then it hit him. "Yeah, first time."

"Glad you're here. Would you like to sign up for a membership?"

He stood there, his face screwed up with most likely a dumb-ass look. "You have to be a member to play here?"

She smiled. "No, no, but you know what they say, 'membership has its privileges'."

He was lost. Was that what Sonny meant…He glanced toward the interior. *What was this bitch talking about?* After a second or two, he found his voice. "What do I get?"

"Let me call my associate, John, and he'll be happy to explain it."

"John?" Fool shook his head. "Nah, that's…"

"It will only take a minute."

His dick could follow that smile anywhere, but his brain put an end to that picture.

"Sorry, not right now. I'll keep it in mind."

Her warmth disappeared as she abruptly turned from him and greeted the next person who came through the door.

He moved off and joined a stream of people making their way into the interior. The dinging sounds of slot machines grew louder after walking what seemed to him half a football field. People who brushed by were dressed to the nines, others super casual, all going in the same direction for the same purpose…money time.

Fool reached the entrance and stood like Moses at the edge of the Promised Land. He surveyed a huge room filled with the desire of getting motherfuck'n rich. *Holy crap.* His eyes widened. The din from the slots and people's screams of excitement were like the steady drum beat from a hard-rock band. He needed to do a recon of the joint. He ambled over the thick carpet wowed by rows upon rows of slot machines spread throughout. Toward the middle of the room were tables for poker and blackjack along with little signs stating what the minimum bets were. In another corner were roulette and craps games. This was nothing like the hood.

He circled the room a few times. *Man, this is awesome.* There was a buzz to the room, nothing like the little shit games he played. He edged toward the $25.00 tables and studied several of them before choosing one. He stood behind the chair of a player, a woman whose arms showed several tattoos.

She glanced over her shoulder. "Move back a step, will ya. I need room.

Fool did as he was told.

"Watch and learn, sonny," she said without turning her head. "Hit me up," she ordered the dealer.

The card put her over "21". "Damn, can't win 'em all." She took a sip of her drink and waited for the next deal.

It dawned on Fool the dealer was using only four decks instead of six that was customary in Vegas. He learned that from various apps. His mouth watered, as the use of two fewer decks made it easier to count. He waited until a particular place opened at the table. He wanted to be at the far end. The last to receive a card.

Fool asked for two hundred dollars in chips as he sat down. The dealer, a skinny middle-aged man whose nametag read Brian, waited until Fool took the crumpled bills from his pocket. Brian spread the money on the table and counted it twice. He then pushed eight twenty-five-dollar chips to Fool and said, "Good-luck". It didn't take long, five deals in about five minutes for his stack to dwindle to three. Can't do much if the cards were fives, twos, and sixes, and the dealer kept catching nines and better.

Fool tapped his pants pocket. He knew there wasn't much left, maybe two Benjamins. *Then what,* lurked in the back of his mind.

Before the next round, Brian rapped his fist on the table and was relieved by a bitch with long hair, long hands, long everything. The nametag, Louise, was clipped on her vest. *Things looking up.*

She didn't smile and was mechanical in dealing. She threw the cards…nine to one, a three, a four to the tattooed lady in the middle and so it went to the six players. Fool got a king, then an ace…blackjack. He breathed a little easier. On the next round he bet fifty dollars. This time she dealt him a queen then a king, another victory. He held the chips in his hand, glanced at the other players, then Louise. Make it seventy-five on the table. The cards came flying at him. He had two tens, and the dealer showed a two. He glanced at the players and the remaining deck.

"Split them," the tattooed lady said.

A quick calculation of probabilities and he agreed and anted another seventy-five dollars.

"Ready?" Louise said.

Fool signaled for the cards. He received one for each hand.

"You have twelve on each. Another?"

Fool concentrated. The noise of the slots and other gamblers faded. It was a rumble between him and the dealer, Louise—mano to mano. He checked the table again and then the dealer's deck. If he hit, he could go over twenty-one, if he stayed, the dealer only needed seventeen to beat him. He drummed his fingers. He had paid attention and believed most if not all the jacks through kings had been dealt that left tens. He took a breath and swallowed. He glanced at Louise who looked noncommittal, almost bored. He touched his pants pocket where his remaining scratch rested. He had played the odds all his short life. What the hell. He signaled with his hand he wanted a card for each. She flipped him a nine on one and a seven for the other.

"Twenty-one and nineteen," Louise announced. She didn't wait to ask if he wanted to hit but dealt herself a three. She had fifteen. She drew another card. "Five-twenty, house wins on one." She swept Fool's chips from his losing hand and paid him on the winner.

Too much pain and not enough gain.

* * *

Anne's hand shook as she laid her phone on the table. "I think Mr. Wilson is as lost as me. He certainly didn't have information. This is shit,

Charise, just shit. I told David. I told him." Her lips trembled as she fought back tears. "I hate it. I hate…" She hit the table with her fist. She caught Charise staring at her. "Frustration, Char, don't worry, I'll pull it together."

"You always do." Charise took a sip of her café latte. "I don't think sitting here is doing you or me much good. We need to do something."

"Yeah, like what?"

"Call your house again, maybe David was on the can or something."

"You think?" She reached for her cell, then shook her head. "No, I called, the sheriff called, there was no answer. Nice try, but David…"

"We have to do something." She looked down at her coffee. "Do you know where Jasmine lives?"

"Uh… maybe it's in my phone." She grabbed the cell and checked contacts. "Damn, only her phone number." She looked toward the ceiling, then at her friend. "I dropped David off once or twice. I think I remember."

"Great. Let's go."

Anne reached for her purse. "Wait. What if Jasmine was killed too?"

Charise had one hand on her hip. "Well…"

"What if it was David."

"At least you'll know."

Chapter Fourteen

J.P. loosened his tie. He didn't think Anne was lying, but then again, she was David's mother. He 'd been in practice long enough to suspect everything. It didn't reflect well on humanity, but given the people he dealt with, it was better that way.

He reviewed the information he had. Fact one: David was gone. No dispute there. He twirled his pen as he thought about what Anne told him. If there was a shooting, why hadn't it been reported? He put his pen down and stared at the legal pad resting on his desk. There could be a number of explanations: the police sloughed it off, or they're investigating but haven't found anything… like a body or bodies. That would make sense.

He swiveled his chair and glanced at the view outside his window. He could see all the way to the lake. On a sunny day, the skyscrapers glistened, and the lake sparkled. Unfortunately, Chicago had days that turned into weeks where it was cloudy and overcast. The view was as depressing as the weather.

If anyone knew something, it would be the cops who covered the beat of the Q and Jerk. He snapped his fingers, turning back to his desk. He'd give his buddy a call who worked the 4th District, then deal with ASA Thomas. He looked up the number and called, using his land line.

"Dietrich, Fourth District."

"Yo D, what's happening, bro?"

There was a pause. "Who's this…J.P.?"

"What a cop. You got it on the first try. What's go'n on?"

"Everything good. What can I do you for?"

"Straight to business…okay. You know anything about a shooting at the Q and Jerk this afternoon?"

"Why would this day be different from all others? There's always something happen'n there. It's a gang-infested miserable joint that happens to have great food if you like hot and spicy."

"Not ask'n about the food, D. I want to know if you guys found any bodies there."

"Like a homicide?"

"Yeah, you're getting my drift."

"Hold on."

J.P. figured D put the phone down as he heard bits of everyday life at the station. After a minute or so, D was back on the line.

"J.P.?"

"Yep, still here."

"Good. Beat 4432 got a call of shots fired at that location. They talked with the manager of the Q and Jerk, but he had little to say. He told them if shit like that happened it was part of the atmosphere of the place."

"Uh-huh. Why hasn't the city shut it down?"

"Not my job, boss. Damn alderman and…well you know the routine. It's the City that works."

"Got it. Did you know the time the cops got the call?"

"Let's see. The transmission of the broadcast says sometime after thirteen hundred; one p.m. for you civilians."

"Thanks for the info, D."

"No problemo. Say, why you interested?"

J.P. picked up his pen and clicked it a few times. "A client of mine has gone missing. Last heard from he was going to the Q and Jerk around that time."

"You got a name?"

"David Lanier."

"Oh, him."

"You know the guy?"

"J.P., he's famous, my man. The kid thinks he's black. Goes by the street name, Fool. Hangs with the gangs. I'm surprised one of them idiots haven't cashed in his number."

"That's what I'm worried about. If you hear anything, give me a jingle."

"Sure will. The way things are, Fool could be resting in the freezer of that joint."

"Nice thought. Don't think I'll eat there. See you."

Chapter Fifteen

"Cash me out," Fool said to the dealer, Louise. "I'm take'n a break.

Louise swept his twenty-five-dollar chips from him. She stacked them in two piles, then gave him two hundred-dollar bills and a fifty. Not great but at least he didn't lose.

"Leaving already?" the tattooed lady asked. "You got to make a day of it. In case you haven't noticed, free drinks to ease your pain as long as you sit."

He checked her out now that he wasn't concentrating on the game. She wasn't bad look'n. He placed her somewhere in her thirties. Her dark hair was shoulder length. She still had curves and a nice rack from what he could tell. Yeah, he thought, she had a few more years and then… Maybe she was like Sonny, a last dance with someone to light up the night. Whatever her angle, he'd save it for later—like dessert. He had money on his mind.

"I'll be back in a bit."

"Uh-huh, you know where to find me."

He weighed his options but was interrupted by a loud cheer coming from the entrance over by the slot machines. Someone was a winner. No better high than coin being dropped in your pocket with no sweat. He knew in his bones even slots had a play. Just had to figure the pattern. He left his almost found love at her table. He was on his way to make his fuck'n fortune.

He joined the growing crowd surrounding the lucky bastard in the "What's Up" t-shirt. The dude kept shaking his head, repeating "Man alive," while re-enacting what he did to win five thousand dollars.

"Excuse me, coming through." Fool moved aside as an important looking bald-headed suit went toward "What's Up".

"Congratulations. My name is Robert Collins. On behalf of the Hard Rock Casino let me escort you to the cashier cage."

"You have my money?"

"It's at the cashier's."

"Naw, I wants it now. I don't know you. I ain't move'n from my machine. I won it and I want it. Ain't go'n no place, no how until I see the green."

"Mr.…?

"You checking me out? Why you want my name and shit?"

"Sir…"

"Don't give me this high-and-mighty crap…"

Fool saw, out of the corner of his eye, movement. *This is go'n to get bad.* He back-pedaled his way through the on-lookers. He was now far enough away from the immediate action but heard "What's Up" screaming, "I have rights," as several big-ass goons headed for him.

That is one fuck'd up dude. Jesus. *What's Up just pissed away five Gs. What a dumbass.* Fool would never allow that to happen. He moved away and searched for a machine. He found another "Wheel of Fortune" and watched a woman pour twenties into it. It didn't take long for "Wheel" to gobble up the money. She left in disgust after ten minutes and at least a couple of hundred down. He was about to make his move when a man dressed in a white shirt took the seat. "I won't be long," he said, "waiting for my old lady. She told me to meet her here." He stuck a twenty into the machine and placed his bet, five dollars at a time. The machine was still hungry. He loaded another twenty and this time he won a little, then gave it all back. "That's gambling for you. First rule: the house always wins." He looked at his watch, then peered down the aisle. "Huh, she isn't here yet. If I stay longer, I'll lose it all. Would serve her right." He stood, "It's all yours. I'll try another."

Fool said, "thanks" and took his place. He had a fifty-dollar chip in his hand and was about to drop it in the slot but stopped. What if he actually won big time like that dumb shit, "What's Up"? They would want his name and address. Not a good thing if he's runn'n from the law. Not a smart play at all. He looked in each direction from where he sat. No one bothered with him. Just another fool ready to feed the beast. At least in cards the odds of winning were better, and no one asked questions.

He wasn't ready to play blackjack again. On his walk over to the slots, he passed the sport's betting lounge. Seemed a little quieter and it had leather cushioned chairs along with banks of TVs. He'd spend a little time there, then hit the tables again.

* * *

"You mind driving?" Anne asked Charise. "I'm too nervous. We can take my car if you like."

"No offense but your old Jeep has seen better days."

"It may be old, but it gets me where I want to go."

"Come on, Anne, we'll be more comfortable in mine."

Anne didn't argue and walked a few steps to the vehicle. "Is this new?"

Charise put her hand on the driver's door handle and unlocked them. She smiled. "Yeah, had it for a few weeks. I'm still learning all the gadgets. I'm hoping one of them can make coffee," and laughed.

Anne slid into the leather seat. "Wow, I get why you wanted to drive."

Charise looked over. Her eyes sparkled. "You do? Wait until this baby hits the road. It's like b-u-t-t-e-r."

Anne buckled herself in. "I bet. Jesus the smell of a new car. Nice." She didn't hear the engine when Charise started the car, and it began to move. "Holy crap. It's so goddamn quiet."

"I know." Charise edged the vehicle into the street. "Where am I going?"

"Let me..." Anne looked at her phone. "Should have thought of the address before. Shit. I think Jasmine lives...hmm...off of... between Jeffery and Stoney Island."

"That's a rather large area, Anne. Narrow it down."

Anne frowned and thought. "I'm trying. Jasmine is...damn...I'll know it when I see it. She's somewhere..." She squeezed her eyes shut for a second or two. "Wait. I think Jasmine stays between Seventy-fourth and Seventy-sixth on either Bennett or Constance."

"Well, that's a little better."

A minute or two passed before Anne spoke again. "Can you turn the radio on to news? There could be an update."

Charise glanced over. "Sure." She pressed a button on her steering wheel and said, "Tune to WBBM AM radio." The radio announcer's voice blared from the speakers.

"Damn, turn it down," Anne had a hand over her ear.

"Sorry, I was listen'n to music, before."

A reporter whose name Anne didn't catch said he was at the Q and Jerk, investigating a report of gunfire. He quoted the manager saying, "Lunch hour very busy. It's possible loud noise but very busy."

"Did you hear that son-of-a-bitch?" Anne asked, "very busy, my ass."

"Calm down; at least no one said anything about dead bodies."

Anne looked out the front window. "True." She dug her fingernails into her palms. "G-d I hate this."

Chapter Sixteen

Jasmine sat back in Big Hit's Caddy. She was tired from her afternoon's exertions and bored with the jive between Big and Short Stuff. All sorts of thoughts rambled through her head. She closed her eyes and feasted on the short film of what occurred minutes before. All those hands on her body and dicks pounding her gave her more pleasure than a year being with Fool.

Why had she remained with him…? Hmm. In junior college, Fool was smart, he got the answers, even did his homework. She knew of him in freshman year. Even had classes with him. Her bitches talked about the white boy who hung around black dudes. One year of school, though, was enough. She didn't go back. She wanted money and got a sales job.

Two or three years later, she spotted Fool on the corner of 75th and Jeffery. She was go'n to catch the bus. Fool was with three other dudes who got nasty. They pawed at her clothes and said how they'd go'n to do her. One grabbed her. Fool stopped them. The boy could talk. His patter went all over. It was hard to keep up. He also had green. Where he got it, she didn't know or care. They went all over—clubs, dances, parties.

It was cool in a dumbass way doing it with a white boy. At first, there was a thrill like someth'n real naughty. Then, when he caught that case… it was sexy. She wanted him bad, seeing him in cuffs and that tan County jail shirt, hang'n his head before the Judge. When he got out on house arrest, they were smoke'n. She was all what her other bitches talked about. They had jealousy in their eyes. Being Fool's woman gave her status. It was all good for a while, but his case dragged on.

Fool lost his coolness be'n cooped up in his crib. He gone stale and with his Momma always around, fucking was more like a number's coloring book than fun. She was too young to stash hip.

Jasmine opened her eyes as she felt the car was no longer moving. She knew immediately where they were. "What the hell, Big? What the fuck we do'n in front of Fool's crib?"

"Shut up. We're wait'n."

* * *

Anne and Charise drove down South Lake Shore Dr. in silence after hearing the newscast. Anne wasn't in the mood for music or Charise's further explanation of the car's doodads. "I'm sure it's great...really... thanks," Anne said, staring out the front window.

She heard Charise humming some—she couldn't place the damn tune. It was driving her crazy attempting to identify the song while worrying over her son. She broke her silence. "What if...Jesus... what if we find Jasmine and she doesn't know?"

Charise stopped humming. She drummed her fingers on the steering wheel. "Well...eh...it solves one of your issues."

"What's that?"

"David was alive but did another stupid... sorry, but..."

Anne let out a breath. "He's not called Fool for nothing."

Charise patted Anne's hand. "Children make us age before our time."

Anne felt her tears forming again. "Yeah...right. Hold on..." She grabbed her purse for a tissue, then looked out the window. They went over the Illinois Central railroad tracks, which meant they passed 71st and Jeffery. A few minutes later she spotted an address on a store front. "We're getting close."

Chapter Seventeen

J.P. held to the imperative of separating his clients' problems from his personal life. "You smile, you listen, you do what needs to be done to represent them. Bring it home? Never." That was the goal, but he wasn't always able.

David Lanier and his mother was a case in point. He became aware it was a strange set of facts after the Laniers came to see him. The unwinding of their version threw up several cautionary flags. A white family that continued to live in a Black neighborhood was not common, particularly in Chicago. That was the first oddity. The second, David's ability to survive even though he ran with the gangs but wasn't quite a full-fledged member. He got through his teenage years with not much of a record, graduated high school as well as two years of junior college. That told J.P. his client either was one lucky bastard or had enough smarts and skill to succeed.

Then there were the crimes themselves. The State charged David with Home Invasion, Attempted Murder, and Armed Robbery. David's story was he happened to be at the victim's crib to buy weed and coke. There was a disagreement over price and amounts. The victim drew a gun that David knocked away, but it went off. David ran out. An unnamed buddy was his ride, but he was nowhere in sight.

Three days later, the police arrested David in his house. A month after the arrest, they claimed they found the victim's jacket, money, and the gun in David's backyard, underneath two planters.

Tasha, J.P.'s secretary, interrupted his rumination.

"The State is on the phone for you."

"Which one?"

"Ms. Thomas."

He looked at the ceiling for a second or two; his grip tightened on the receiver. Instead of picking it up, he pressed the intercom button. "Tell Ms. Thomas I'll call her back in a few minutes."

"Okay."

He leaned back in his chair. From experience, J.P. gathered there was more to it than what David told. His story, from J.P.'s point of view, had a lot of holes. Despite his doubts, he took the case. At the time, J.P. felt the fee quoted would more than make up for the aggravation. Experience, though, should have taught him: the money rarely does.

He also violated his rule; he grew fond of his client and his mother. Theirs was an intriguing story. Both he and David grew up near each other but in different eras. They went to rival high schools but knew the neighborhood spots. J.P. was luckier, though. His family was stable, David's tragic. The loss of David's father left a void his mother, Anne, worked hard to fill. At least David had someone in his corner, unlike many who had no one.

J.P. looked at David's thick file lying on his desk. He thought back to all the interviews he'd had with him. J.P. pressed David on the gaps in his story. Over time, David became a little more forthcoming.

His client swore he never took anything from the victim's house. There was never any gun, jacket, and money in his backyard. The way he put it, "It's not like California. There's rain, snow, and shit. Duds and coin get moldy and the rod, hell, the exposure ruins the piece." David had a point.

J.P. ordered the weather reports of the time in question. It had rained the first two days after the "robbery", and the rest of the month was cold and cloudy interspersed with a few sunny days. When he inspected the evidence there was no mold and the gun appeared to be in good working order. Most important were the arresting cops. He had a growing suspicion they were dirty based on his research of prior complaints and lawsuits against the two. Nora, J.P.'s lunch date, confirmed it.

J.P. reached for the file. He took a deep breath. Such a waste of all the hours he spent investigating and planning, along with a few sleepless nights. Now David disappeared—all gone to hell.

* * *

Fool relaxed as he sat in one of the plush chairs watching a bank of TVs that had every kind of sport imaginable. He marveled at the sleek and sultry servers dressed in black blouses and matching short skirts asking if he'd like a beverage. *Holy shit, what a way to live.* He ordered a rum and cola and gave the hottie a dollar tip upon delivery. She slipped the bill in her waist band and smiled as if he handed her a Franklin. He thought he had found heaven.

"You play the horses, my man?"

The question snapped Fool out of his reverie. "Huh?"

"You've been watching the Hialeah races since you sat down."

"What?" Fool's drink splashed against his hand as he set it down. "Hi...a...I...I...races? No man, I..." The man didn't seem threatening, though. He was dressed in a white shirt that badly concealed a fat belly, a beard... and he spoke funny.

"It's okay. Look, if you have some sort of system for betting on the horses...not my business. You don't know me, so there's no reason to tell."

Fool's hand never left his drink that rested in its holder. "I'm not betting. I'm...just... What's it to you, anyway?"

The man rubbed his beard and shrugged. "Nothing. I saw you sitting so intensely. I thought maybe... you knew something. This kind of betting, to tell you the truth, not for me." He took a step closer and lowered his voice. "It's all fixed." He waved his hand. "But cards, that's something else. You can do something—more control."

Fool wondered if he was being played. The man's rap didn't match the look of a card shark gambler. He took a sip of his drink. Fool was deliberate, taking his time before responding. "So, cards your game?"

The man's eyes brightened, and he sat down next to him. "Cards are a series of probabilities that by using math determine the winners or the losers."

Fool must have had a "hangdog" look as he caught some of the man's drift. "Say what?"

"There's a system for everything...even cards. That's what I'm saying. Learn it and you'll fill your pockets."

Fool did a quick check of the man's trousers. "You talk the talk, but I don't see..."

The man grabbed his wallet from his back pocket. "See these hundreds?" He flaunted several of the bills.

"O-k-a-y?" Fool still not sure whether this homie was blowing smoke. "What do you want from me?"

"From you? Nothing." The man looked away for a second and glanced at the TVs. The picture on the screen must have gotten his attention.

Fool followed his gaze and saw his photo with his arrest number flash on the television. He froze. He didn't hear what the newscaster said. He sat rigid. *It couldn't be*, he argued. That wasn't him. He slowly turned from the monitors and stared into the face of the bearded one.

"You look like you could use a meal. Come."

Chapter Eighteen

Jasmine got pissed. What the hell did she get herself into? Excitement, holy shit, yeah. What a relief from the boredom of being chained in a manner of speaking to Fool's house and bedroom. She was happy to fuck Fool; she giggled at her joke. It was another if Big had ideas to do him in. She wanted no part of that. She leaned forward and cleared her throat. "Come on, Big, whatchagot to do with Fool no more. He's history."

"No shit," he grunted and kept his eyes on the house. "Sit back, bitch. You crowd'n me."

She saw his neck muscles twitch. "Okay. Didn't mean noth'n. Fool probably ain't even at his crib. He wouldn't mess with you—not after the Q and Jerk." She sat back and twisted the gold chain of her purse.

"Call him."

"Call? You want...why the fuck...? You gave your word. I did what you wanted. All your homies had their fun. Right, Short Stuff?"

Short Stuff glanced at Jasmine from the front passenger seat. "Big the man. Do what he says."

She looked from Short Stuff to Big for any further reaction. There was none. She did a quick calculation. The life she led with Fool was gone. She didn't miss it, at least not yet. It felt so alive to be giving and getting so much pleasure. Big ain't go'n to do something stupid. He too smart...although...?

She dug into her purse. "I'm search'n." She felt her eyebrow pencil, lipsticks, condom package. "Jesus."

"Come on now. Quit stall'n," Big ordered.

Short Stuff grabbed for the purse. "Give me that."

"Get your ... I got it."

"Make the call," Big said.

She dialed Fool's number. "What do I say?"

"Ask him if he's at his crib. You want to talk to him. Tell him to come out."

She stared at the back of Big's head, then viewed Short Stuff who still had his eyes on her. *This ain't right.* She sensed Short Stuff gett'n ready to jump over the seat to get beside her.

"Put the screen where Short Stuff can see."

She held it up.

"She's call'n him... Big."

The cell's connecting sound filled the car until Fool's voicemail picked up.

"Hangup," Big said.

She punched End. "Okay, we cool now?" She waited for an answer. "You listen'n?"

Big turned to face her. "Girl, you mind yourself. Your mouth go'n and I'm not interested in what you got to say. You're here for one thing... pussy. Now as long as you understand, everything cool, and you'll get more coin and shit than you ever had in your life. There's noth'n more to it. We're staying here a while longer. Now shut up before I let Short Stuff use your mouth for someth'n else."

* * *

Charise turned right on 73rd Street and then a left when she came to Bennett. "We're close to Seventy-fourth."

"I'm looking. Drive a little slower."

"I would if I could but someone behind me is almost up my ass."

Anne shifted her glance to the side mirror. "Jesus, what's that guy's problem?"

"I don't know but I ain't go'n to find out." Charise stepped on the pedal and put distance between them.

Anne wondered if that car had anything to do with Jasmine and David. She could feel the thumping in her chest as she weighed that idea. She asked herself; *how would anyone know*? She wasn't even in her jeep. But what if... no impossible. Why would she be followed? She had to calm down and keep a check on her imagination. For G-d sakes, this wasn't TV or a movie. She eyed the side mirror and saw the bastard now was several car lengths behind.

"Charise, forget about finding Jasmine. I don't think I can figure out which building. They all look alike. Besides, it was at night when I dropped her off. Let's go to my place."

"You think David is there? Really?"

It took Anne several seconds. "I'm aware of the reality, maybe he left a note... something. I need to hold on to..."

Charise finished Anne's sentence: "Hope."

* * *

J.P. hit the intercom and asked Tasha to get Assistant State's Attorney Thomas on the phone. He had put it off as long as he could. He prepared himself for an earful by reaching into his lower desk drawer and retrieving a bottle of 12-year-old Macallan. He scanned his Baume & Mercier watch for the time: 2:10 p.m. *Never too early.* He got a glass out of the same drawer and gave himself a good pour. *Here goes.* He tilted his head a bit and got a taste. *Damn that is good stuff.* He viewed the glass and the deep reddish color of the liquid still in it. Smooth as a virgin ice rink. Jesus, that's perfection.

"State's Attorney Thomas, line one." Tasha brought J.P. back to the present.

He picked up. "Joclyn, J.P., what's cooking?"

"You don't know?"

"Know what?" He kept his voice playful.

"J.P., are you putting on one of your 'oh shucks' routines? You're not in front of a jury. I'm calling about your damn client, Fool."

"What about David?"

"Stop bullshitting. You know damn well. I left a message with your office. I'm also telling you there's a warrant out for his arrest."

"What a surprise."

"Whatever compelling story your client had, is gone. Tomorrow I'm filing another complaint for escape, and it will be consecutive."

"Joclyn, you're getting ahead of yourself."

"What do you mean?"

"First you have to find him, then convict."

"Don't play smart with me, J.P. Your client is throwing his life away. I'm going to hit him with everything we have."

"Aren't you taking this a bit personally?"

She paused. "Maybe. I don't like being lied to."

J.P. tightened his grip on the receiver. He weighed his words carefully. "I didn't do that nor did David. Your hope that David would be the entry into the gangs was a possibility, not a promise. I made that clear to you."

"Whatever, J.P.," her voice retreated, "I'll send you notice of the State's Motion later today." A few seconds went by. "Find your client." She hung-up.

J.P. dropped the receiver into its cradle as he reviewed the conversation. No doubt Joclyn was angry. Not uncommon for a state's attorney but it was more like David or he himself betrayed her. Or was there something more? Something he didn't see. That was always the worry. He shifted to the Macallan's that awaited him. Unlike his business, there was nothing hidden in this scotch. What you saw is what you got—perfection.

Chapter Nineteen

Fool at first didn't hear or maybe understand what this overweight, funny-looking dude said. Eat? Food wasn't on Fool's radar at the moment. *What is this man's game?* The dude hadn't moved nor had Fool in the seconds after the telecast. Fool's inner voice screamed he had to ditch him but despite that, Fool sat, paralyzed, his brain in hyper mode spewing thousands of scenarios leading nowhere. Like that Shakespeare dude the line popped into his head, "...a tale told by an idiot filled with sound and fury signifying nothing." *Where the fuck did I pick that up? Honors English. Mr. Campbell. I'm los'n my goddamn mind.*

This stranger had soft eyes. A smile crept across the man's face. He gave Fool an I-mean-no-harm look. Fool didn't get it. He was sure the dude saw and heard the same TV monitor. Fool was wanted by the p-o-l-i-c-e and yet that news flash didn't seem to faze the dude.

"Nah," Fool finally spoke, "ain't hungry. I think I'll move along."

The dude seemed to look past him. "Yeah? Where? Your secret," he glanced at the TVs, "not much of a secret, is safe with me. We'll pretend I didn't hear or see it. What do you have to lose?"

"You a cop? A narc? Some law dude?"

"Me?" He laughed. "The last thing in the world I'd ever be. No, son, I'm not."

"I don't get it. Why you doin' this?"

The man pointed to the casino area. "You came here to bet, to make money...yes?"

Fool shifted his view to where the dude pointed. He shrugged. "Yeah, I guess. I figured I'm out of Illinois."

"Well, I'm proposing a sure thing, something you don't get here. Like I said, you have nothing to lose, and you'll get a meal out of it."

Fool considered the proposal. "You're not a cop," he asked for reassurance.

The man shook his head. "No, again." He began to walk.

Fool unconsciously followed. "Where are we going?"

"I know a place. I'm known as Rabbi Sam or Sam. My mother and father, *a-lv-h-a-shalom*, lingo for rest in peace, would pronounce the name as Sem. Europeans."

"Huh? Rabbi?"

Sam stopped for a moment. "Don't worry, I'm not, just called that by some folks, like preacher or reverend." He didn't say anything for a moment, then continued his march through the casino.

Fool's jaw dropped. The dude's a rabbi? Crazy, makes no sense. Too many questions, but what was his choice? He spotted several security guards, checking out the crowd, then saw the back of Sam's white shirt weave through the throng. Ain't noth'n to do but follow. *Jesus.* Shit. *Can I say that? Don't want to disrespect the dude, er, Sam.*

They neared the entrance. Sam was in front and Fool a step or two behind. A cop stood to the side of the same lady who stopped Fool a few hours before.

"Hurry back," she said looking at Fool as the two of them passed her on their way out.

He caught a glimpse of her for a second. "Sure will," and then avoided further eye contact.

The wind had died down, but the chill remained as Fool and Sam stepped outside. It was that hour where the last bit of daylight unwillingly surrendered to the encroaching night. Fool looked up at the sky and watched the colors change from a glowing red to purple to not quite black. He took a peek over his shoulder. The signage of the Hard Rock stood out against the growing darkness. No one followed. They headed toward the parking lot, its security lights beginning to shine. They walked down one row of parked cars, then another.

"Don't you know where your wheels is?" Fool asked.

If Sam heard, he didn't respond. He kept walking, then stopped, looked at the vehicles in the vicinity, and continued down the line of cars to the next.

"What the fu—. I mean, whatchadoing? What are we looking for?"

Sam held up his hand. "When I see it, I'll let you know."

"Shit, there's thousands of cars. Are we going down every row?"

"Boychik..."

"Say what?"

"It's an endearing term like 'my man' but in Russian/Yiddish. I'm looking for a car that fits our station."

"You're...what?... You... boosting a car?"

Sam looked down the row, then at Fool. "Boosting? Are you accusing me of stealing? What precisely do you mean?"

Fool couldn't tell whether Sam was jiving or serious. Sam didn't move. He stood there waiting for Fool to answer.

"You know, taking something not yours."

"Ach...good...good. Now this taking would be forever? Or, what if it was for a minute or an hour and I returned it."

"Man...I don't know. You givin' me a headache. I don't need no more trouble."

Sam glanced down the row, then returned to Fool. "No trouble. You assumed I was taking something not mine. You assumed wrong. I'll find what I'm looking for."

Fool looked around. The coldness of the night was seeping through his clothing. He shivered. "Where? What?"

Sam went down the line of cars, then pointed. "This one."

Fool strained to see the vehicle from where he was; too many were in between. He caught up to him. Sam stood by the driver's door.

"Is this yours?"

"Go around to the other side and get in."

Sam moved his hand over the door latch and the doors unlocked. "What are you waiting for, boychik?"

Fool didn't have an answer. If the dude opened the door without a jimmy the Jaguar must be his. Or... damn the cold. He patted his money pocket...so what. The sum wouldn't take him far, and he was getting hungry. He went around the back of the ride. There was no license plate. Shit. Did Indiana need one? He heard the engine start. Sam must have the keys or something. He opened the passenger side and caught his breath...slick. He smelled the newness of the leather. The dash console looked like something out of an airplane, although the only one he'd seen was in a video game. Fool got in. "This really yours?"

Sam pulled out of the space and rumbled toward the exit. "Ain't she a beauty. I've wanted one all my life." Seconds later the car peeled onto the street. Fool was pinned to his seat. "Jesus."

Chapter Twenty

G-d knows how long they be outside Fool's crib. Jasmine wanted to ask how much longer they go'n to sit and do noth'n, but she kept her mouth shut. She put one leg over, then the other. She needed to pee. All that fucking worked on her bladder.

"What's wrong with you, girl?" Shorty asked.

She hesitated a moment and then said quietly she needed a bathroom.

Big grunted. "Why didn't you go at the Q? Can't be helped at the moment."

She wanted to remind him she'd been a little busy taking care of his crew. But he knew that or should. Didn't want to rile him. Hell, she needed to get what he promised: paid. It was fun and all, but green was green. Cash, baby, snow, or glitter; however, he wanted to dole out the stack. She knew, Big knew, she did good. Better than good, she was hot as a firecracker. She'd be in demand.

She saw him check the driver's side mirror. "Car pull'n up. Look like the law come check'n on your boy."

Jasmine turned in her seat to look.

"Sit straight, bitch."

She quickly obeyed. "He ain't my boy. How many times I tell you."

Big didn't answer. He tilted the rearview mirror. "They park'n a few spots down. Look at that. Some dude in plain clothes and a woman wear'n a jacket with 'sheriff' written across the back, cross'n the street and going to Fool's crib. This is go'n to be awesome. Fool's ass being dragged out. What you think, bitch? Are you gett'n worked up?"

"Did you forget already? Fool ain't there."

"We go'n to make sure now."

Big rolled down his window a bit. They watched the man ring the doorbell, then saw him pound on the door. The sheriff bitch had a hand near her hip, probably resting on her piece.

"Shit, you think they go'n to break that down?" Shorty asked.

"They make'n enough noise." Then Big shook his head. "Nah, they'd bring more pigs to do that. It's a meet and greet, but nobody answer'n. You right, Sugar, Fool got his white ass out of there."

"Great, can we go then?" Jasmine pressed against the passenger door, her hand between her legs. "I gotta pee, Big. Can we go?"

"You hold on a bit longer. Want to see what they do next." Big turned to Shorty. "Where you think Fool's momma be?"

"Don't know. I hear she be fine. Ain't that right, Jazzy?"

Jasmine turned toward Shorty. "Never looked at her that way. Why you want her, anyway? She old."

Shorty had a smile from ear to ear. "Same like you had Fool. She white."

"You a dog," Big laughed, "but you have something to it. Never had a white piece of ass, myself." Big looked out his window. "Guess the law is leaving. Momma got to be coming sometime. We'll stay put." He glanced over at Jasmine. "Here's an empty cola can," he lifted from his cup holder, "piss in that."

* * *

Anne let the word "hope" play in her mind. It gave her the same feeling when as a little girl, her father kissed her on top of her head. "It'll make everything better," he'd say. It would for a while, like wishing for Santa only to realize there was no Santa or Jesus, or G-d especially after Sol hung himself. She rubbed her hands and let out a faint *hmm*.

"What was that?" Charise asked.

Anne looked over at her friend. "Nothing, just thinking what bullshit 'hope' is." She sighed. "You get all worked up clinging to…to a belief, a vision, and then step through the door and reality slaps the shit out of you."

Charise glanced at her. "You a downer, Anne Lanier. Not the same woman I know. You a fighter, always have been. Even though you're a little thing, you have more guts than ten people put together."

"You're making me blush."

"No, for real. I don't know what I'd do if my man did that and left me with a child and a mountain of bills." Charise turned back to watch the road. "You picked yourself up, turned your husband's clothing business into a success, and somehow kept an eye on David."

"Not much of an eye. I wasn't around. David grew-up without me."

"Ain't true. You were there when he needed you. The rest was his choice. You showed him the right way. You were an example, but he was too…sorry to say it, stupid to see."

"David, David." Anne made a *tsk tsk* sound. "Ever since his case started… I don't know… we ran out of words. He and I existed in the same house and barely talked. And if I had something to tell him, Jasmine lurked behind him like an unwelcomed shadow. I lost control, Charise, over him, my life, his…" Anne buried her head in her arms and took several deep breaths, then looked up. "Sorry, it's a G-d damn mess and who knows if it will get better."

Charise reached over and patted Anne's shoulder. "I ain't going to say it will be all right. Whatever it is, you'll have the strength to fight it. That I know. Now tell me where to turn. I forget."

Chapter Twenty-One

J.P. finished his drink and decided to move on from the Lanier matter. He had other cases, and there was nothing more he could do until David was found and re-arrested. It was too bad for him and his mother just as the tide was turning in David's favor, but shit happens. He hit the intercom button.

"Tasha, do I have anything more on my schedule this afternoon?"

"Let me check."

He heard her rustle papers, then she was back. "Nope. You have court tomorrow, Judge Sembrow at Belmont and Western."

"Thanks." He hung up.

Out of habit, he patted his stomach. "Ugh", took a breath, and decided. He'd work-out at the building's fitness center. The membership cost enough and if nothing else, it would clear his head. He got up from his desk telling Tasha on his way out where he was going.

The elevator to the top floor was fast and silent. A soft bell announced the destination. He stepped out, walked a few feet, then opened the massive wood doors of the fitness center. Floor to ceiling windows behind the receptionist area circled the entire center. What a view—sheer beauty. A portrait of a great city on the shores of its lake.

A very fit young lady sat behind an acrylic desk and greeted him. "Good afternoon," she said in a sultry voice. "Will you be working out with us?"

J.P. could have been flippant and remark what his id wanted to say, but instead he nodded, showed his card, and headed to the locker room with the vision of that woman stuck in his mind. He'd be doing himself a favor to come more often. There'd be a chance he'd learn her name, and everything else about her.

For the price he paid for the privilege of membership, he had a private locker with his gym equipment cleaned, folded, and ready for him to wear. He changed quickly in the nearly vacant locker room, grabbed a few towels, and headed to the exercise area, thinking about the pain he was about to inflict on himself.

He started on the treadmill and set it for twenty minutes. He raised the setting to where he was jogging. In the hood, where he grew up, the idea of paying to exercise would be a joke…outright crazy. The laughter would ricochet from one apartment to the other. He'd hear his father.

"Boy, you want exercise; get muscles? Go play ball and if you want more, work at the mill like your old man. Hell, an hour or two at the plant, you wouldn't need anything else. Promise you, boy, your body would ache for a week. Exercise my ass. What the hell wrong with you? Paying good money for that shit." Yep, that would be Pops. Well, times changed.

J.P. used one of his towels to wipe the sweat from his eyes as he turned up the setting to a full run. He lasted two minutes before dialing it back. The machine then took over, lowering the speed as his twenty minutes was nearly up. When finished, he stepped off the treadmill, his legs momentarily wobbled. A woman reached out and stopped his fall.

"That's embarrassing," J.P. said, straightening himself. "Thanks, that never happened before. Don't know how…"

"I was waiting for the machine—guess right place right time." She let go of his arm. "You all right?"

"Oh yeah. A bruised ego, nothing more."

She stepped around him and got on the tread.

"Careful with it," he warned.

She glanced over at him. "I've been on it many times. We're sort of friends."

"Okay." He eyed his next machine. "Thanks again."

She leaned forward and pressed Start. She started to walk. J.P. turned toward the next challenge.

"Simone," she said as her pace quickened. "You work in the building?"

"I do. You?"

"Fifteenth floor. Jenwick, Dyson, and Barney. I'm the Jenwick part." She was now at a slow trot.

"Lawyers?"

"Not on your life—merchandise brokers."

She raised the level and was now jogging.

"What kind of…"

"Clothes, mostly. We provide a service to the mom-and-pop stores."

She caught her breath. "We buy their close-outs and then sell to other buyers."

"Huh. Nice niche."

"It's a living." She upped the tempo and was at a full run. "I've.... seen you... someplace, before." Her words came out in bursts.

"The elevator?"

"No...no..." She glanced at him. "TV–that's it. You're that lawyer...J.P. Wilson."

"I am."

She slowed down to a trot. "Yeah, you're on that case...something about...I forget, but I know that kid's mother."

"You do?"

She slowed to a fast walk. "Done business with her."

"Hmm. How about a drink after we're done here."

She glanced at her watch. "Tell you what, I'll meet you at the downstairs bar at five."

He checked the clock on the wall. "Great. See you then. I'll go torture myself over there." He pointed to another set of machines.

"Don't hurt yourself." She quickened her pace back to jogging.

* * *

J.P. returned to his office. He stepped lightly, ignoring his muscle's rebellion. His newfound friend, Simone, had made anticipation work better than Advil. She was easy on the eyes, seemed smart, definitely fit, and to his good fortune agreed to have a drink. It was "all good." He walked past Tasha who had her coat on and was about to leave.

"Anything I need to know, Tash...baby?"

She gave him a-what's-got-into-you look. "Naw. Oh, Nora called."

"Nora? From the State's Attorney's Office?"

"Yeah, I guess. She didn't give me all that. Just said her name and number." She gave him the slip of paper with the information.

"Thanks. Have a good evening."

She glanced at him, smiled, and seemed to want to say something more, but instead reached for the door. "See ya tomorrow."

He wished her well and went into his office. He closed the door and dropped into his chair behind the desk. Nora. Jesus, what a time to call... did the corned beef sandwich he gave her this afternoon go bad?

He punched in her number while checking his watch. Fifteen minutes. He hoped this conversation wouldn't take long. She answered on the third ring.

"That was fast," she said.

"Whatchamean?"

"I only called ten minutes ago."

"Oh..." he paused, "so...eh...what's cooking?"

Nora lowered her voice. "You know those two cops we talked about...Sanchez and Klinaire? There's more 411. Can't really discuss it...here..." she paused and, in a whisper, "how about meeting for a drink or dinner. I get off at five."

Simone's image flashed through J.P.'s mind. He was tired of the Lanier shit. *Oh, to be done with it, but...* "Okay, okay," he glanced at his watch. It was five to five. "I'll tell you what, I'll meet you say six-thirty at Topol Gigio on Wells."

"Six-thirty?"

She didn't sound happy. "Sorry, I can't leave before six. Have a drink or something."

"Forget it. I'm doing you the favor, J.P."

He arched his eyebrows. If fate calls, he knew he should answer. "Nora...Nora...you know I appreciate..."

"Cut the bullshit, J.P. Word gets around, you know."

"Oooh, that hurts. How long will it take to pick me up at my office from Twenty-sixth Street?

"Now you talk'n. I'll see you in forty-five minutes. Be out front." She hung up.

Fate is twisted.

Chapter Twenty-Two

A smile crept over Fool's face as the Jaguar accelerated. *Jesus, this baby can fly.* In the two to three seconds, it took the car to hit sixty and beyond, the velocity freed him of his troubles. The past put on hold. He reveled in the power. Then, like one of them movies that shows the action in slow motion, the thrill vanished as the car slowed for the brake lights of the truck up ahead. What the hell was he doing? He snuck a peek at Sam who seemed to be concentrating on the road. He still didn't know what was up with him. What he did know was no one does somethin' for nothin'. There's always a price. Fool sized him up and figured he could take him if he tried anything funny.

Sam interrupted Fool's thoughts. "What do you know about cars."

He gave him a blank stare. "Whatcha mean?"

"Besides the obvious, what do you know… take this one, for instance."

Fool did a quick check of the interior. "Like it's hot. Never been in a ride that smells so new."

"Not what I'm getting at. Do you know the make and model?"

"Yeah, it's a Jag convertible, and I guess it's a '23 or '24."

"Uh huh. Who makes it?"

"I'm not stupid, Sam. Jaguar makes it. That's a dumb question."

"Actually, the company is owned by an Indian corporation called Tata."

"Say what? I thought it was…huh…They're in James Bond…he was English. It's English."

"Originally, but Jaguar had been bought and sold a few times. Ford even owned it for a while."

"No shit…Ford? Can't see that."

"You just learned a valuable lesson."

"I did? What's that?"

"From the questions I asked."

Fool waited for Sam to say something more. He brushed his hand through his hair and leaned into his seat. Sam stayed silent. Fool had enough. "Man, you talk in riddles. You're messing with my head. Aren't we only having a conversation? Didn't know there's a test involved."

"Your anger is from confusion. Think about the line of questions I asked. Your responses were natural, easy, and on the surface correct. But people ask questions not only to hear the obvious. They ask to find out what you know and to learn your ability to analyze. Like a quarterback who not only sees the first receiver but also the entire field. Capiche?"

Fool drew a breath. "What the fuck, Sam. You play'n with my head." He glanced out the window and, in the distance, saw a large blinking neon sign…*Café Bineto.* Sam turned into its driveway and parked in a secluded place.

"Hungry?"

Fool waited a second or two. "Let me think on it…I'm hungry and that's all the football field I see."

"You're catching on. That's good. Let's grab a bite."

They entered the restaurant. Several couples were waiting for a table, but Sam acted as if they didn't exist. He made his way, dragging Fool with him, to the front, no excuse me or any of that shit. He spoke to a dude dressed in a dark suit and bowtie who stood near the entrance of the dining room. Sam spoke softly and fast. Fool didn't catch the words. The bowtie man called another guy dressed in a dinner jacket, said something, and dinner jacket disappeared outside. A few more words were exchanged between Sam and Bowtie. Bowtie nodded and led them to a table in the corner, even though the joint was filled with people. Not any people but fancy ones—suit and tie and long dresses, fancy. A waiter, also in a white shirt and tie, brought them menus and said something to Sam…sounded foreign…hell… Italian? *This is out of my league.*

"What did you say to bowtie dude?" Fool didn't wait for an answer. He patted the white tablecloth, looked at the tile floor, then the walls filled with art. "This ain't go'n to be cheap." He opened the bill of fare. "Holy shit. What is all this stuff?" He dropped the menu and pushed himself from the table. "I don't have the kind of green for this."

"Sit down. I told you I'll take you to dinner. Don't worry about the prices. It's on me."

Fool hesitated, then fumbled for his seat. He leaned toward Sam. His voice louder than conversational. "I've had it with your game. What do you want? What's the price I'm go'n to pay?"

Sam put his forefinger to his mouth. His eyes darted from Fool to the surrounding tables then back to Fool. "I'm offering you a meal. If you don't want it…leave. There's nothing more to it."

Their eyes locked for two or three seconds while Fool considered whether he should stay or go. Sam gave nothing away. Fool was no match for Sam, besides Fool's stomach growled. "Okay. I'll stay, but if you…"

"What are you talking about?"

"You know…" Fool said quietly. "Funny stuff. I ain't into it and…"

Sam laughed. "You think I'm interested in…please. You're…" He rubbed his face. "Is that what you were thinking? My G-d, shlongs, dicks to you, not interested. Got it?" He motioned for a waiter. "You like red or white?"

"Red or white, what?"

"Wine."

Fool shrugged. "…whatever."

* * *

Jasmine turned away and stared out the passenger side window. Her insides went cold as the realization of her role in Big's world got real. She and Big weren't going to share power. She wasn't going to be some queen who gets to choose who'll receive her sexual favors. Her pussy will be opened to whomever Big decides when he decides. He may throw her some green, or snow, or glitter, but it's on his terms. Piss in a can. She ain't no animal…a dog on the street.

"You can keep that cola can," she says to Big. "I'm read'n you loud and clear."

"Don't give me no attitude, bitch. Think beyond yourself. We do'n a job. Got to stay ahead of what's behind. See what momma do'n. Ain't that right, Short Stuff?"

"You right like you always is. Don't want momma to hurt us none. Got to see what she up to."

Jasmine continued staring out the window. It all sounded good, but they had evil in their hearts.

Big held up his large meaty hand. "Hush, now. A ride pull'n up. Does momma drive…what's that…hmmm… SUV…Toyota?"

Jasmine twisted around to get a look out the back window. "She drive a beat-up bluish Jeep…it ancient."

"Jesus, girl, sit straight. We don't want whoever that is look'n at us. Check out the side."

Jasmine obeyed. "Don't see noth'n. Hold on…the driver…she too tall, it ain't her."

"What about the other one com'n alongside."

Jasmine gasped. "Yeah…the short one. That's Fool's momma." She could hear a smile in Big's voice.

"Get out."

"Whatcha gon' do?"

"What I say. Tear up. Tell her what Fool did to you."

"Huh?"

"He fucked you, baby. You ain't lying. You just didn't want him to this time."

"What?"

"Do it, bitch. We ain't play'n. Momma is gett'n near the front door. Move your ass." Big turned to face her, pointing his Glock. "Now you be all drama and we'll let you have fun, later. Move."

Jasmine's hand shook as she opened the door. She took a peek over her shoulder as she got out. Big had the rod pointed at her. She took a step, then another. "Momma Lanier," she called out and worked some tears. She saw Lanier turn toward her.

"Jasmine? Is that you? My God, I was so worried."

Lanier came closer. She was about fifty feet from Jasmine. Her friend, the taller one, didn't move from the front door.

"Are you all right?" Lanier asked and took another step.

The sound of ear-splitting thunder exploded, then two more. Jasmine fell to the ground.

She came to lying in the backseat of Big's ride listening to Big and Shorty laugh.

Chapter Twenty-Three

J.P. gathered the files he needed for the next day, threw them in his briefcase, and grabbed his coat. It can all work-out—a get-to-know-you drink with Simone and who knows what with Nora. The evening was full of potential.

It wasn't the first time he'd had two dates on the same night, and it wouldn't be the last. The key… be yourself. In court, jurors sensed when an attorney took on a personality not his own. Same was true with women on dates. It's a cadence of when to listen and when to talk. The right emotion at the right time. He took a deep breath. Timing…life's secret to success.

The elevator to the first floor was crowded with people departing work. The mass of humanity leaving their how-I-make-my-money life for their spouse or single life. That's why bars existed. The doors slid open on reaching the first floor and he made his way through the throng to the restaurant/bar at the front of the building. The noise of dozens of conversations hit him as he opened the door. J.P. knew the hostess, Liz, well. It was hard to miss her as she was clad in a black jacket and skin hugging black pants. Her long blonde hair was a magnet. She greeted him and asked if he was staying for drinks or dinner. He had to shout to make himself heard.

"I'm looking for Simone Jenwick. She works in the building. You know her?"

She pointed to her left midway down the bar. "I think that's her."

J.P. looked. He wasn't sure. The woman seemed taller and older. Her dark hair wasn't in a ponytail but fell beyond her shoulders. She looked so much more professional than she did in the gym.

"What the hell," he told Liz. "If it isn't her…" He left with a smile as he navigated his way.

She was standing holding a drink surveying the scene. He immediately noticed her black blouse and fitted beige pants. "Simone?"

Her smile let him know he picked right. "I hope I haven't kept you waiting long."

She moved closer to him and put her hand in back of her ear. "What? I'm getting too old…not used to the noise."

J.P. held up his hand. "I'll see what I can do." He pushed his way back to Liz. "We need a table. Somewhere a bit quieter."

She patted his arm. "You gotta be kidding. It's cocktail hour."

He gently touched her hand and discreetly dropped a twenty in her palm. It disappeared into her pocket.

"For you, J.P.…." She smiled and grabbed her walkie-talkie. "I'll have a table for you in a minute or so. Go get your damsel du jour."

"Come on, Liz, I'm not that bad."

She looked him up from head to toe. "No, indeed."

"Thanks," and he battled back to Simone.

"You're a drink behind, J.P." She pointed to her glass. "What's your poison?"

He got within inches of her and shouted, "There's a table waiting for us. Take your cocktail and follow."

"What about the tab?"

"Don't worry, we'll straighten it out once we're seated."

A few minutes later, Liz led them toward the rear of the establishment. People were dining and the roar from the front ebbed. "Enjoy," Liz said as they sat down.

"You think she works out," Simone asked as soon as Liz was out of earshot. "What an ass!"

"I didn't notice." J.P. grinned.

Simone rolled her eyes. "Yeah, nice try. I don't know if I ever had a rear like that. I keep working, though."

"I'd say you do well. You certainly know your way around the gym."

She took a sip of her drink. "Nice of you to say."

"No, really. First thing I observed." He leaned a bit closer.

She held his gaze. "My, my, you are smooth. Whatcha drinking?"

He put his hand in the air to call a waiter's attention. It didn't take long.

"Yes sir, I'm Michael and I will be taking care of you today. What can I get you?"

"Macallan 12, neat."

"And for the lady?"

"Jack and Seven," her eyes twinkled, "more Jack than Seven."

The waiter nodded.

They each had a few more drinks. Actually, they lost count of that and the time. This was too much fun to… Their voices no longer discreet, often interrupted by spurts of laughter. If he had to recount their conversation, it was full of life's stories, nothing particular except one. He had asked her about her business, and she brought up Anne Lanier. They must have been in between drinks. J.P. had nursed the urge to check his phone to see if Nora called, but when Anne was mentioned, he forgot.

"How do you know Anne Lanier?"

Simone raised her eyebrows. "Known her most of her life. We went to school together, even stood up at her wedding."

"It's a real shame what happened. Her husband committing suicide and all."

Simone picked up her empty glass and ran her finger around the rim. "I probably shouldn't say this, but…what the hell, you're defending her kid."

"I'm all ears." He signaled for another round.

She snuggled close to him. "Sol wasn't her husband. Legally yes, but…"

The waiter came and refreshed the drinks.

J.P. stared and for a moment was speechless. "Holy shit," he finally muttered. He grabbed his glass. "Here's to…to…"

"Secrets."

They clinked glasses, then burst out laughing.

J.P. didn't remember who suggested another place but was agreeable. The bar had emptied, by this time. Liz still manned the reception podium and gave J.P. a subtle wink.

"The garage is through the lobby." He guided Simone to the door.

The car jockey brought J.P.'s Lexus. Simone whistled, "Nice," and climbed into the passenger seat. J.P. tipped the kid and got in. "Where do you want to go?"

Simone's eyes sparkled. She wetted her lips and brushed her hair back with her hand. How about something audacious? "My place."

He slid his hand over the steering wheel, maintaining the impression of being relaxed and cool, even as he struggled to hide the sense of victory bubbling inside. "Where's that?"

"Not far. I have a townhouse on Seminary near Fullerton. You good to drive?" She looked over at him.

"Oh yeah, I'm fine."

She nonchalantly positioned her hand on his thigh.

"Even better."

Chapter Twenty-Four

"Man, whatever this stuff is," Fool held the wine glass to his mouth, "I'm stoked. Best I ever had."

"You're drinking a Barolo. Legend says it was the grape for kings. What would you drink?" Sam asked.

"Wait a minute, you say'n Eminem the king of hip hop drinks this shit?"

Sam's eyes widened. He appeared flustered. "Who? Never mind. My point was this grape was reserved for the upper class."

Fool looked at his dinner partner and chuckled. "Huh." He sat up a little straighter. "I drank whatever...Boones Farm, Ripple, Mogen David..." He could see disapproval in Sam's face. "Hey, if you have enough other shit, you're flying just the same." He used his arms to imitate a bird's flight.

Sam shook his head. "Not the purpose of wine. You can get high on anything, but this...it's to complement what you eat. It brings out flavor the food didn't know it had."

"Huh? Damn, you're so serious. Lighten up. I'm mellow. This stuff, the wine... It's like...like, man it's almost better than sex." He sloshed the wine in his glass. "I take that back. Fucking and ..." He circled his arm around the table. "That's boss. Yep, boss. If my woman saw this...man." He used his hands to tear bread from the loaf, then buttered it. "Never had something this good. I could eat the whole damn thing."

"Save room for dessert." Sam sat back and adjusted his napkin. "What about your woman? Does she know you..."

Fool stopped chomping. Why not tell him? Hell, it was because of Jasmine he ran. He didn't owe her shit.

Sam waited for an answer.

The wine hadn't totally fogged Fool's brain. He could still think. Could he trust Sam? Buying a meal was one thing, giving him 411 about himself, another. He gave Sam a long look, while his hands fumbled with part of the uneaten bread slice. *No man, I still don't know Sam's game.*

"I ain't talk'n about that," Fool said, grabbing his glass. He guzzled down the last of his drink.

"Suit yourself. I'm sure she'd like this place. It's hard to find a better Italian restaurant."

Fool was all smiles. "You got that right."

Sam glanced at the dessert menu. "We'll have tiramisu."

"What's that? Sounds Jap like."

Sam made a face. Shook his head. "Boychik, have you lived under a rock all your life?" He was about to continue but the waiter interrupted and took their dessert order. Once he left, Sam leaned forward. "Sorry, I shouldn't have said that. Probably a lot of folks your age don't know and hadn't had the chance. Hell, at your age, I wouldn't even have guessed it was Japanese."

"Then why did you say that crap?"

"I…I got ahead of myself. Sometimes one forgets what it's like to be young. Look, I don't know much about you except what I saw at the casino and that news clip. But I sense you have a head on your shoulders. You have street smarts. I like that—better than book smart."

"Yeah…whatever."

The waiter served the desserts, interrupting Sam again. "Would you like coffee?"

Sam nodded. "Make that a cappuccino, and one for my friend."

"Sugar and cream with that, sir?"

Sam glanced at Fool, then said, "Sure. Bring both."

The waiter left to prepare the request.

"What the hell did you order? A cappa…what? Was that mafia talk for…"

Sam picked up his fork. "Try the dessert but eat slow. I ordered a special kind of coffee. It complements the tiramisu."

"Ain't you a man about town. You got it all down. You have a woman, Sam?" Fool took a bite. "Jesus, this is the best shit." His fork shook while he held it over the plate. "I…I…Sam does everyone know about this…tiramatsu?"

"Tiramisu," Sam corrected.

Fool dug into another piece and had it inches from his mouth when the waiter returned with the cappuccinos. He placed the service on the table. "Will there be anything else?"

Sam told him, "No", and the waiter left.

Fool gazed at the white foam forming a pillow at the top. "It's a small cup, for coffee. How much do they get for this?" He rested his fork on the plate."

"Not your worry. Sip it, then take a bite."

He did as Sam suggested. "G-d damn." He caught his breath and couldn't get over the bombardment of sweetness, cream, and coffee taste in his mouth. "Does everyone know about this stuff?"

Sam had helped himself to a piece. After he swallowed, he admitted the dessert was good.

"Good? You outta your mind. This…this is…gold. If I sold this in the hood…" Fool slapped the table.

"David, if this was blackjack, you're holding sixteen and the dealer is showing a ten. The Italians have been making this for a long time. The world knows about it."

"Yeah?" Fool gazed at the delicacy on his plate, for a moment. "Okay, maybe so, but not with the dudes I hung with. They have no idea. We'd clean up. I'm tell'n you."

"You're saying this would be the new grass, the new snow?" Sam calmly ate another piece of his dessert.

"Why not. The hood knows noth'n about this. I'm proof."

Sam took a sip of his cappuccino. "You may have something, boychik. I'll think on it."

Fool eyed Sam as he finished his tiramisu and coffee. *Maybe, Sam is good people.* Maybe, some kind of door was opening and maybe Fool was no fool. He digested those thoughts. A warm feeling settled over him. His mind wandered.

Damn, if Jasmine was here. She'd look at him as the 'man'. Jasmine. She was his woman, and he didn't do noth'n knowing she was having her brains fucked. Were those dudes for real or had she set it up? G-d damn, he left her and his momma and now he had this crazy idea…tarama…whatever. Shit. It would never fly. Another dumbass thought in a long list of them.

He saw Sam still enjoying his dessert. What the fuck was his game?

Chapter Twenty-Five

Blue flashing lights and siren screams pierced through the haze of Anne's partial consciousness. One minute she was outside her house, the next—searing pain, then blackness. There was something over her mouth and cheeks. She couldn't tell what it was, but it felt good…like her face had its own air conditioner. Sketchy voices similar to a radio where the dial wasn't exactly on the station played in the background. She picked out, "U of C" and wondered what the hell…? Why there, for God's sake? Why anything? Why everything?

Her mind spun and that word, "why," tumbled round and round. David…David…why did you go? Jasmine came. Jasmine, there's someone behind you. Jesus, even with that air on her face, her mouth … so dry. Sol. The garage. Her body stiffened. *I shouldn't have, but I did.* Swing you bastard, swing.

Her mouth so, so dry. A male voice… "racing…blood…" Something pricked her arm. A coolness swept over her.

She heard water and saw herself on a beach. A man lay next to her. It felt so warm. She sat up and admired the palm trees that were near. She listened to herself say something to the man. She put on her sunglasses. There was something hanging from one of the branches. She got up. Her pace quickened. "No", she shrieked, "David? My poor little boy."

Did she scream? Was that her, her voice?

Hands. She felt them. Her eyelid forced open. A light so bright, she had to catch her breath. Danger. Jasmine didn't come alone. Was that a gun? Oh…Charise…Charise…no…oh.

Another prick and the scene vanished. The light extinguished and she drifted into a heavy darkness…warm… peaceful.

* * *

Big watched as Shorty did his work. The instant Shorty got Jasmine into his ride and slammed the door; he hit the gas. The tires screeched as Big flew down several streets, ignoring stop signs. He checked the rearview mirror after several blocks, then slowed down. No sense attracting eyes when it needn't be.

"Them white bitches caught one hell of a surprise." He laughed. "I seen it all."

"You right, Big. Jazzy here got them all confused. Never saw me comin'." He joined in the laughter, careful not to outdo Big.

"How many rounds you get off?"

"Come on, I hit the trigger and let it fly. I emptied the load. Pretty sure got them both."

"Well, Shorty, you might have earned a reward. Ain't that right, Jasmine? Think he worthy?"

She didn't answer.

"She agree. Shorty, you lucky bastard. She be all yours when we get to the crib."

Big glanced in the mirror. Shorty was smiling from ear to ear, his hands groping Jasmine's legs. "Shorty, keep your dick in your pants. We still have things to do. Besides, you'd want your woman cleaned up a bit. You know what I'm say'n."

Shorty stopped feeling her legs, but not before he squeezed her thigh. "Yeah, I'll keep it in my pants. Don't you worry. I'm workin' up an appetite. You hear, Jazzy. You goin' to put out like a bitch in heat. What else we got to do?"

"Get rid of the rod. We'll go by Rainbow Beach and Jasmine will toss it in a can."

"You got it all planned out. You good on it, Jazzy?" Shorty nudged her foot.

Jasmine struggled to open her eyes. She could feel her body shaking. They shot Momma Lanier. Big and Shorty used her. She didn't like Fool's momma, but killing her? No way.

She was in deep, deep shit. They wanted her prints on the gun. It will be her ass, not theirs if the p-o-l-i-c-e find it.

All she wanted was a good time—a little freedom, that's all. Now she's in with these crazies and that little punk drooling all over her. Not the ticket she signed for.

It took her some to get the energy to sit up. She felt the little shit hit her foot. She glared at him.

"You almost killed me. You asshole. Why…why…?" She fought back tears, which would be the last thing she'd want the two bastards to see.

"Murder." She hit the back of Big's seat. "Damn y'all."

Big wheeled his ride to a side street and stopped the car. There were few houses and even less cars. He got out and opened Jasmine's door. He grabbed, then pulled her out.

"What are you doing? Stop." She was woozy from the sudden movement. Big's hand was like a vise on her shoulder.

"Move." He kept her from falling and marched her to the passenger side away from the road. "Get on your knees." He pulled his gun from his jacket and pointed it at her head.

* * *

J.P.'s Pop was fond of saying, "Drinking and women lets you forget your troubles until the morning comes." J.P. didn't know why that phrase popped into his head. The evening with Simone was going very well. He turned the car down the darkened street of Fullerton Parkway.

"I'm two doors west of Seminary. Pull into the driveway." Simone took her hand off his thigh.

The brownstone building looked regal as he eased to a stop. "Hell of a nice-looking place. Always was impressed with these homes."

"If you're good, I'll let you see the inside."

He leaned toward her, and they kissed. "How's that?" he asked when they broke apart. Even in the dark he saw her eyes sparkle.

"It's a start."

He followed Simone as she opened her front door. His shoes made a clicking sound on the marble floor in the foyer. Somewhere deep in his subconscious his old man fiddled with a warning light. Why? She hadn't acted in any manner that would give caution.

Simone flicked on the lights and led him further into her home. She seemed sane. She certainly had a figure that was health club certified. Meeting up and all was her idea. Hell, she invited him. Nah, it was out of caution Pops was knocking around his brain. That was him. He'd always look over his shoulder, make sure the coast was clear. Damn.

They came to a staircase. "There's a bar on the lower level. Help yourself. I'll join you in a minute or so. While you're there, make mine a bourbon with a splash."

The bar was no small affair. It seated at least seven or eight people. He took inventory of the stock of liquor standing at attention on the glass shelves. It was top of the line. Any tavern would be envious. A bottle of Angel Envy stood out. From what was left, it must be one of Simone's favorites. He found a glass underneath the bar and gave her a good pour the way she ordered. He set her drink on the dark wood top, then searched for scotch from the selection behind him. The Macallan's bottle seemed to have been hiding behind two others. He swayed, almost losing his balance as he went to get it, no harm done. He took a breath and held the bottle out to examine. It was one of them cask jobs with no mention of the whiskey's age. *What the hell, it's Macallan's. How bad could it be?* He found another glass and gave himself a healthier pour. Just in case, he found ice in the bottom fridge and dropped a cube or two. Sacrilege for a connoisseur, but in his mind there's a discount for drinking something that didn't provide a clue to its vintage.

He heard Simone over the intercom. "Would you be a dear and bring the drinks. I'm on the second level."

This could be the beginning of... Second level? Jesus, this is one big ass house. J.P. handled the climb carefully. No need to show off his klutziness, although it was an effort. This second staircase wound in a spiral. The cubes rattled in the glasses as he reached the top. There was a light at the end of the hallway, which he presumed was coming from a bedroom. *No bullshitting and getting to know you, for her. Down to the nitty-gritty. If that's the way she wanted to play it, that was fine with me.* He quickened his pace.

"I'm down the hall." She came to the doorway in the same clothes she wore at the beginning of the night.

He hid his surprise and brought the drinks as if he was in a club and was the gallant one who fetched the refreshments. "I tipped the bartender on the way up." He smiled at his little joke and handed Simone her bourbon.

"I hope it was a good-size one." She held her tumbler in front of her face. It partially hid her smile. She took a sip. "Excellent." She moved into the large sitting area of the bedroom. He followed and was dazzled by the décor. "Holy crap." A thick Persian rug took most of the floor. Large tapestries covered the walls. There were two expensive-looking chaise longues on either side of a round glass table in the middle. Opened French doors guarded the bedroom. *Am I in the Orient? The home of some pasha.* "Quite a place." J.P. sat opposite Simone.

"Yeah, the house was in sad shape when I bought it. I did a lot of fixing up. It took a couple of years, but now…it's home."

J.P.'s gaze flicked around the room. "Must have cost quite a sum." He drank some of the scotch. The way it went down told him he did right using ice.

An uneasy silence settled. J.P. subtly eyed the area beyond the French doors and wondered if they would get there.

She put her drink on the table and stretched out on the chaise. "You know there's room for two on these things."

"Really?" He put his glass down on the table and joined her. He sat on the edge. His gaze went from her face down her body. "I guess so."

She scrunched a little, making more room for him. "Why don't you get closer?"

The request was like the bugle announcing the start of a horse race. He was ready. She was too. In between passionate kisses, she whispered she wanted him to be rough. "If clothing gets in the way, tear it. Rip my bra. I want you to take me…. hard."

If that's what she wanted, hell, he'd oblige. He didn't have a history for that kind of performance but there was always a first time. He tore her clothes and bra. The heat of the action rose in him. He wrestled with his belt as Simone pulled his shirt.

"Hold on," he gulped and sat up. He quickly did away with his clothes.

She rested herself on her arm and watched for a second or two, then sat up and placed her arms around him. "Let's do it on the rug. More room."

The thought of a bed flashed through his head, but then who cared. She was on fire and so was he. She tugged on his dick, panting "nice," and guided it into her. Thrusts from him and squeals from her built toward a crescendo. He felt her fingernails on his back. He wasn't going to last much longer. A thousand thoughts streaked across his brain to stave off the inevitable but nothing dissuaded nature's will. He came and she…she seemed to still be going. He tried to keep up for a few more strokes but that wasn't the way God made man. She opened her eyes and furled her brow questioning for an instant. "Shit… You mind?" She let go of him and he took her hint and rolled off. He stared at the ceiling waiting for his breathing to return to normal.

Simone slowly rose and picked up her clothes. "Well, these are shot." She held out her panties and bra. She took another step. "Aw, the blouse is too." She gripped them in her hands and brought them to her breasts. "I think you should leave." She dropped her clothes, then moved toward the French doors. "It's late. I'm sure you know your way out."

He stared at her. Morning's coming.

Chapter Twenty-Six

Sam pushed back from the table. "Now that was a meal."

Fool put down his cappuccino and agreed. He wondered what came next now that his belly was full. "What time you got, Sam?"

"It's early…about nine."

"We've spent two hours eating. S-h-i-t. Don't think I ever did that." He leaned closer. "Not even fucking…two hours!"

"Some things require it, others, not so much. The two you mentioned, to do it right, shouldn't be rushed."

"Come on, Sam, you can last that long? You take'n me for a ride."

Sam dabbed his face with his napkin. "Suit yourself. It's not just the act but what leads to it. The dessert comes at the end of the meal for a reason."

"You are the king of bullshit, but I like it. You've got an answer for everything."

"I'll take it as a compliment."

"So, what's next? You drop me at some corner and it's I'll see yah?"

Sam seemed to look through him. He shook his head. "Is that what you think. I fatten you up and then throw you out. You got me wrong, kid. That's not what I do."

"Hey, didn't mean anything by it but that's the way life goes."

"Really? What are you…all of twenty-four or -five? That's the world you live in?"

Fool fiddled with silverware, stacking them one way, then the other. "What do you know of the hood? Nothing stays from one day even to the next hour. You got to keep ahead of what's comin'." He reached for his almost empty cup. "It's like that dude in… what was that movie? Flying carpets and Arabi…*Aladdin.*"

"*Aladdin?*"

"Yeah, the dude sings someth'n like stay'n one step ahead of the sword. You know what I'm talk'n?"

"I…how do you know from…"

Fool shrugged. "I hear things. Radio is free." Sam didn't appear convinced. "Okay, my old lady took me to see it. I was a kid, then, but the song stuck."

"That's how you live? You're missing out on a hell of a lot."

"Maybe so, but I'd rather be do'n than sitting around figurin'. I hardly know you, but I got a feelin' that's what you like to do…think…plan. Ain't got the time for all of that."

Sam took a sip of his water. He smiled. "Not ready to go yet. There's a finishing touch to a great dinner." He raised his hand and caught the waiter's attention.

"What's that…the bill?

Sam waved the comment away. "You'll see."

The waiter approached. "Yes sir. Will there be anything else?"

"Two Sambucas and the check."

The server nodded and left.

Fool felt Sam's gaze. The pause in the conversation made him fidget. If Sam wasn't dropping him on some corner, was he getting ready to call the cops? What's sambuc …whatever. Italian for the heat?

The waiter returned with two glasses of a clear liquid. He also placed a leather folder near Sam. "Salud," he said and left.

Fool stared at his drink. "What's these three things floating on top."

"They're coffee beans."

"You shitt'n me. Why the hell?" He grabbed the glass.

"Don't—" Too late. David had taken a gulp, resulting in a coughing fit. "Take some water." Sam gave him a glass.

Fool gained control and sat back in his chair. "You try'n to kill me? What the fuck, Sam."

"You were too fast. I was about to warn you but you, eh…acted before…"

"Shut up." He stared at his drink. "What is that stuff?"

"It's an Italian liquor. You sip it. Really."

"Man, that set my mouth on fire."

"Go ahead. Try it the way I suggested."

Fool grabbed the glass and brought it to his mouth. The smell of licorice made him hesitate. "Nah, I don't think so." He put the drink down.

"You're missing out." Sam raised his glass and drank slowly. He smacked his lips. "Good stuff. Warm you all over."

"I bet." Fool shifted his weight in his chair. "I'm ready to get. My ass is glued to this seat."

"No problem." Sam reached into his pocket and slid three Franklins into the leather folder.

"How do…you never looked at the bill."

Sam pointed to his head. "I've been here enough. I know."

Fool admired that cockiness in Sam. The amount didn't faze him…like he was buying a pack of cigarettes. Jesus, who the hell was this guy?

"Where to?" Fool stood, waiting for Sam to join him.

Sam got up and said something to the waiter who swooped up the folder with the cash. "Have to talk to the maître d' for a moment. Wait for me in the lounge. I'll meet you there."

Fool found a seat at the bar and ordered a beer. At least he knew what he was drinking. Bits of conversations flew around him that he ignored. His attention was drawn to the three TVs hanging on the wall in back of the bar. One had a basketball game, another Fox News, and the third had the local crap. He scanned all three, but the local one caught his eye. He left his seat and moved closer. He heard the reporter say something about a shooting. Fool immediately recognized the location. T*hat's outside my house. Shit.* He stood rock still. The reporter droned: "Two women had been shot. One was dead on arrival at University of Chicago Hospital; the other was in critical condition. Their names have not been released."

Fool staggered. His heart raced. He heard himself yell but didn't know what he said. Someone tapped him on the shoulder. "Son, you all right?"

"Sam. Sam, I got to get home."

Chapter Twenty-Seven

Jasmine squinted at Big. His ivory-handled pistol was still pointed at her head. She wasn't afraid. It was like watching a gangsta TV show. It was happenin' to someone else…not her. She heard the click of the hammer being pulled back. Her life didn't flash before her eyes. The insane thing was she thought of Fool sitting in a classroom and she doing her best to get his attention. She giggled.

"You think this is funny?" Big stared at her. "You laughin'?"

"Huh?" She looked directly at him. "I guess I am."

"I'm about to blow your head off."

"If you give it a moment…yeah. I did your homies. Gave them the best fuck they ever had, passed your crazy-ass test without complaint. Now you have me, down on my knees and you want to blow me away. It's so jacked it's funny."

Shorty opened the rear passenger door. He stepped to the curb. "Come on, Big, Jazzy didn't mean anything…"

"Get your ass back inside. This has noth'n to do with you."

Shorty retreated and shut the door but rolled his window down. "Say you're sorry, Jazzy. Apologize."

She looked over at Shorty. Damn ridiculous that little shit wanted to be her savior. "Shut up, Shorty. Didn't ask you for help. If Big wants to off me…well…get it over with. I can't stay on my knees forever. Least not to get my head blown off."

Big had to hand it to the bitch. She had balls. If he didn't shoot her, he'd be disrespected. Shorty will think, if he thinks at all, that Big gett'n soft. Can't have that. The bitch has to be taught a lesson. He took a few steps back and checked out the road again. No cars. "Shorty, get out here."

Shorty opened the door and stepped out.

"You got your piece?"

"It's in the ride."

"Get it."

Big turned to Jasmine, who was still kneeling. "Get up."

Her knees felt they needed oil as she slowly stood. "Now what?" She put her hands on her hips more to steady herself than for defiance.

Shorty joined Big several feet from Jasmine.

Big smiled. "Take your shoes off."

"Take my...what the..."

"I ain't play'n. Do it."

She struggled to stand on one foot, then the other. "Okay, they're off."

"I'm going to give you a ten count, then Shorty will start shooting."

"What? I don't want...Come on, Big... please...she didn't mean noth'n."

Big shifted his gun hand toward Shorty. "It's either you or her, Shorty. You can always get some pussy."

Those seconds between Big and Shorty gave Jasmine her chance. She took off toward Big's Caddy like the devil was behind her. She pulled the driver's door open and jumped in. Dumbass Big left the motor running. She floored it.

Big glanced over to where Jasmine had been, then saw his ride move. "Hey, what the fuck..." He pulled the trigger and sprayed several rounds.

* * *

Annie get your gun. Anne it's a hard knock life. The tunes from those musicals played in Anne's head—one after the other. It was her own personal Sirius radio with only two Broadway shows. The music suddenly stopped, replaced by the cackle of radio transmissions. It was still dark wherever she was, then she realized her eyes were closed. She struggled to open them and after a few seconds succeeded. Air, cold air attacked her, and she was moving. *Whoosh*! A sliding door opened. The wheels of her chariot clattered. They were moving fast. Voices, commands, a corridor, then another, someone shouted, "Hurry." Another *whoosh* and hands grabbed her, lifting her onto a table. Something went over her face. Her music started again, then faded until there was nothing.

* * *

What happened? J.P. hadn't formed that question until after he climbed down Simone's damn spiral staircase in his socks with his shoes and coat in hand. He did a two-step on one of the stairs while pulling and zipping up his pants and prayed he wouldn't tumble to the bottom. He tightened his belt with his free hand, checked his back pocket for his wallet, then the front for his keys…so far so good. He stepped into his shoes outside her front door. After that he slipped on his coat and immediately realized his tie was somewhere other than on him. He settled into his car and sat in the driver's seat. His attention was drawn to the second floor of Simone's house. Her light was on. He kept watching. What more was there to see or hear? His gut told him to get the hell out. The girl was nuts, but the notion hadn't coordinated with his brain. What was he hoping for? She'd change her mind?

He reviewed the evening, searching for signs he missed. *Desire obscured the subtleties, Mr. Defense Attorney.* He drummed his fingers on the steering wheel. He wasn't stupid, nor was he a kid. Hell, this wasn't his first time with a woman. He could tell the difference between someone who wanted it and those who teased. She had her hand on his thigh, for God's sakes. She invited him. His fist struck the center console. He quickly glanced at the indentation and hoped he hadn't ruined it.

What's your defense, counselor? He came up empty. He'd plead she was a crazy-ass bitch, knowing it wasn't much of a defense at all. Jesus, Pops was right. He should have listened. "Tear my clothes." Wasn't that a flashing red light? Should have been, but a hard dick has no other purpose or thought.

The light turned off in Simone's second floor window. He better get. No telling what she'd do. He started his Lexus, flipping on his lights after clearing her driveway. He drove a few blocks, then pulled over to check his phone. "Oh shit." Seven missed calls from Nora. The last was at eight, needless to say, several hours ago. He didn't hear a one. Should he call? What was his excuse? He never meant to stand her up. He sighed. Choices. He'd lecture his clients about the situation they found themselves in because of… all right, he was guilty, guilty, guilty. He checked his watch… well after a proper hour to call. At least it bought him time. He flicked on the radio to the news station WBBM and began his drive home. The announcer recited the weather, early traffic report, then local news.

"Two women were shot on the far southside. One was dead on arrival; the other, identified as Anne Lanier, is in intensive care at U. of

C. hospital. The police have no one in custody."

The story jerked J.P. out of his self-absorption. The issues of his social life vanished, replaced by this sudden shock. He snapped into lawyer-trial mode. *Who would do such a thing? David?* The thought clung to him. *Why? Was there an argument between them?* He took a deep breath. *David didn't seem that kind of person…shoot his own mother. One really had to be cold and cruel-hearted. What about the gangs? Wasn't that why David took off?* He turned up the sound for the radio, hoping to learn more, but the announcer went on to other news.

He passed the exit for his house without thinking. He had to see Anne. This shouldn't have happened to her. She had enough tragedy in her life. Then again, the son of a bitch who tried to kill her may also have something to do with David and his case. So many loose ends dangling to unanswered questions.

J.P. grew tired as he squinted from the blur of city streetlights. The liquor and his evening's exertions may also have contributed to his growing fatigue. He switched the radio station to Broadway musicals. As he listened, his old man came to him again. Pops used to say, "Life don't fit in no pretty boxes." He sure got that right.

Chapter Twenty-Eight

Fool blinked and realized the man who asked if he was all right wasn't Sam. "Sorry, I thought you were someone else. Gotta go."

He raced out of the lounge to the front of the restaurant where the maître d' had been stationed. The son of a bitch wasn't there. Fool felt beads of sweat forming at his hairline. He peeked inside the restaurant. There were several diners left but no maître d' and no Sam. *What the fuck.* He put his hands in his pants pockets and felt his small amount of cash. If he had to travel, he had enough to get back to Chicago. He spotted the waiter who served them cleaning off a table and went over to him. Fool forgot the waiter's name. "Hey. You seen Sam?"

"Excusi?" He straightened.

"Sam, you know. We sat over there." Fool pointed.

"Sam?"

"The dude who paid in cash."

The waiter shrugged. "My English...not so good. Sorry."

I bet. You had no problem when we ordered. Fool stared. "Really? You don't know what I'm saying?"

The waiter had a blank look. "Excusi. I finish my work."

Fool felt the impulse to push the dude against the table and rearrange his face but held back. "Yeah, fuck you, man." Fool walked away and returned to the front where the maître d' had been. He strained his neck to search. Two or three couples milled about, but Sam was nowhere in sight. *Maybe Sam went to the head.* Fool tapped a man helping a woman with her coat.

"Say, you know where the john is?"

He pointed down the hall.

Fool took two to three steps in that direction before mumbling, "Thank you". He got to the men's room and pushed the door open. No one was inside. He stood over a sink and ran some water to splash on his face and wipe away the sweat. He caught his reflection from the mirror that hung above the basin. It scared the hell out of him. His eyes were red-rimmed, and his hair splayed in several directions. He grabbed hold of the sides of the sink and pressed his frustration and fear into his grip. Seconds passed as his arms shook from the pressure he applied. He let go. Time was wasting. His mother could be dying or dead. Who was the shooter? It had to be Big or some other asshole who ran with him. It was Fool's fault. He stayed too long. Thought he was hot shit and too cool to be messed with by his so-called brothers. Wrong. Wrong about everything. And Jasmine? Was she part of it? He shook his head. She wouldn't. Nah, that'd be too cold even for her. Besides, she may be gone too. Big could have had his fun and then… Can't worry about her. He had to get back to Chicago. Sam, the son-of-a-bitch, where was he? The thought hit him. The car…the Jaguar. Did Sam take off?

Fool bolted out of the bathroom to the front of the restaurant. The maître d' was still missing. He ran past and out the front door. The parking lot was dark, but the streetlamps gave off enough light to see. He trotted to the spot where he thought they'd parked. The space was empty. He wildly searched in one direction, then another. "Sam, you out here. Sam…Sam?" Fool smacked his hand. He kicked himself for believing the dude would help. "Too good to be true. Motherfucker!" He shouted that. A pair of headlights caught his attention coming from the rear of the building. He stood still, listening to the roar of the engine. The lights of the car sped toward him, nearly blinding him. He put up his hand to shield his eyes, then jumped aside as the damn thing raced past him, through the lot, and exploded onto the street. Fool followed its movement and recognized the shape of the vehicle. It was a motherfucking Jaguar.

* * *

"Dang, you shot me, Big. You shot me." Shorty's hand dripped with blood after covering his shoulder wound. "I'm bleeding." He stood several feet from Big.

Big's Caddie, though, was halfway down the street. He charged after it, firing his piece as he went. "Jasmine, you bitch. Come back here." After the third or fourth shot, the car careened into a tree.

"Aww, shit. The bitch messed up my front end." He hurried over to examine the damage. It looked like the tree got the worst of it. He went over to the driver's door with his rod in hand and threw it open. Jasmine was slumped over the steering wheel. *Thank Jesus she didn't fuck up the airbags.* He stood for a second or two, figuring if she was dead or alive. It didn't matter one way or the other. He was go'n to throw her ass out. He holstered his gun, but before reaching in, he heard trudging feet.

"Big, I need help. Big..."

Big drew his gun. Shorty was comin'. "You're make'n too much noise..." Damn fool. "And bleed'n all over the place. You'll mess up the car." Big straightened. His finger slid over the trigger. "Can't have that. You're go'n to put your bloody hands all over my interior. The ride got to be clean inside and out."

Shorty kept move'n closer. "Guess you ain't hear'n straight." He fired and hit Shorty in the head. "So long, Shorty. You know it had to be this way."

Shorty crumpled to his knees, then fell over. Big, dragged Jasmine out of the car and dropped her close to Shorty. "Well, Shorty, you get to fuck her in heaven," he snorted. He wiped the handle of his gun with his jacket, then pressed Jasmine's fingers on the butt and trigger. He positioned the weapon inches from Jasmine's outstretched hand. He checked his work. Two bodies lying in a darkened, nearly deserted street. "Hmm. Roadkill," he laughed, then climbed into his ride, carefully picked several pieces of glass from the dash, and drove away.

Chapter Twenty-Nine

J.P., unshaven and bleary-eyed, trudged through his office door. Tasha looked up from her computer. The top button of his shirt was unbuttoned.

"Where the heck you been?" A smile played at the corner of her mouth. "Oh boy, you been up all night. You still young enough to be do'n all of that?" She shook her head. "At your age? My oh my, you be the man."

"Yeah, yeah. If you must know I've been to the hospital. Anne Lanier was shot last night."

"Oh?" Tasha's smile vanished. "I thought I heard somethin' on the evening news. Is she…"

"The pricks wouldn't let me see her. I'm not kin. Thank God I knew one of the cops. Unfortunately, he didn't know much more than what was reported. He did tell me they think two were involved. One may be a woman."

"A girl? Jesus, have mercy. What's this world comin' to? What about Ms. Lanier?"

"I stayed until around seven, then I had court. The nurse said she'd call when things stabilized." He took a breath. "So?" He looked at Tasha.

She spun around in her seat and reached behind on her credenza. "You got messages." She grabbed a bunch. "None were from a hospital." She handed them to him. "Two of them were from Nora James. Don't think she believed me when I explained you weren't in."

He raised his eyebrows and held onto the phone slips. "I need coffee."

"Yeah? The machine is where it's always been. Oh, I almost forgot, Simone Jenwick said she'd stop by later toward noon. Says she's in the building."

"Hmm. Did she say anything more?"

Tasha rubbed her temples. "No, don't think so. She didn't sound like it was any big deal."

"Interesting."

"Is it a big deal?"

"What...No... I met her yesterday at the health club. Probably wants to go work out or something."

Tasha returned to the computer. "Like I say, Mr. Wilson, you the man."

J.P. went into his office and shut the door with his foot. Did Simone have a change of heart? He settled into his chair and stretched his back. Damn. Simone. Last night her fingernails must have gouged his skin. He felt a dull burn that became more pronounced when he moved. He winced and promised to check it out later.

Did he have her all wrong? He grabbed a ballpoint pen off his desk and squeezed the top. The soft clicking sound echoed through the room. Maybe it was just the price to pay for passion.

He checked the time. It was 11:15 a.m. He better call Nora before she becomes a full-blown crisis. He needed as many allies in the State's Attorney's office as possible. He took out his cell phone and dialed. She picked up after two rings.

"How dare you stand me up. I called you several times. Who do you think you—"

"Good morning to you, Nora."

"I don't want to hear your bullshit. I can't believe—"

"Nora, please. I was at the hospital."

"There you go again. You were... where?"

"Hospital. Anne Lanier was shot last night."

J.P. looked at his phone, making sure they were still connected. "Hello? Nora?"

"The mother of your defendant? Shot? Oh my God. Is she...?"

"Don't know. I was there until around seven this morning. The nurse said she'd call, but I haven't heard."

"Huh. Sorry." He heard her breathe into the receiver. "I'm still pissed. I hate being alone at a restaurant bar. I didn't know what happened to you. I thought one of your clients could have..."

"Can I make it up to you?"

"I should say no. I'm still angry. "But you owe me."

"I do. Sorry for messin' your..." J.P.'s intercom button lit up. "Eh, Nora..." Seconds later his door opened, and Simone walked in. "Call you back."

Chapter Thirty

Fool watched the taillights of the Jaguar disappear. He took a deep breath. In the hood, that's the way life goes. Things happen and too much think'n only gets you into deeper shit. *Fuck you, Sam, and all that bullshit about seeing beyond the moment. Ain't much I could do about you take'n off even when I thought it might happen. At least I got a meal out it.* He took one last look around the parking lot and walked toward the restaurant. He reached the driveway and heard a car approach. He stepped to the side without looking.

"Boychik, get in."

Fool stopped. A Mercedes with the passenger-side window down was next to him. The voice was unmistakable.

"What the…?"

"Get your ass in here. There's news on the radio that may be of interest."

Fool leaned on the passenger side door. "About my old lady?"

"Could be."

"I know that already. I went lookin' for you, then saw you drive off. You're a son of a bitch, Sam. I'm going back to Chicago. Don't want nothin' to do with you."

"Boychik, you thought I left you stranded in the middle of nowhere. Stop thinking the worst. Get in."

Fool straightened. He slid his hand over the passenger door. It was smooth and clean.

"Where's the Jag?"

"Will you get your ass in the car."

Fool did a quick glance, wondering if the cops were on Sam's tail. Everything seemed normal. "Look, I can't get pinched at the moment. Is this ride hot? Where's that maître d'? What ain't you tellin' me?"

"You sure ask a lot of questions." Sam peeked at his outside mirror. Fool could see him checking things out.

Sam turned back to Fool. "There's nothing funny going on. The cops aren't coming. Now, if you want to stand out there and pray you get to Chicago, that's your business. Make up your mind, 'cause in a second or two I'm leaving."

Fool held onto the door while looking toward the street. There were no cop cars coming and he didn't hear any sirens.

He rubbed his eyes. It'd been a hell of a long day. He stole a glance at Sam. He sure as hell looked like he owned the world. The bastard was a mystery man. That's who he was. Whatever game he had goin' seemed to be working. If this was Blackjack, Fool had sixteen and Sam's top card showed a king. The odds told Fool to hold as Sam had the upper hand. Fool got in. He eyed the back seat before buckling his seat belt and felt Sam's stare.

"Lookin' for someone?"

"Just make'n sure it's just you and me."

"Want to check the trunk? That's the way the Mob does it." Sam popped the lid. "Satisfied?"

Fool didn't get out of the car. He figured no one in their right mind would open the damn thing if a body was inside. He shrugged. "Yeah. Now what?"

"You have to be smart about this, David. Going willy-nilly to your mother's hospital bed will have you in cuffs before you could say your mother's name."

In Fool's mind, he thought surprise would save the situation. His hands became clammy the more he thought about it. Wrong again. God damn. He was earning his nickname. He glanced at Sam. "All right, what's your plan?"

"Don't have one yet, although staying in Indiana is a hell of a lot safer than Chicago. Whether this is a trap or not, you'd be walking right into it by going to the hospital."

"A trap? We both heard the story on the news."

Sam patted Fool's arm. "Boychik, sometimes what we hear are lies. Call your girl. Maybe she knows something."

"My…? Nah…bad idea, Sam…no way."

"Okay. Guess I touched a nerve."

Fool slunk deeper into his seat. He was fucked anyway he went. Couldn't see his old lady, couldn't call Jasmine, couldn't show his face in Chicago. He scratched his cheek, then his head. "Hey, what about my mouthpiece. Can't I call him?"

"You mean your lawyer?"

Fool returned the stare. "Yeah, that's what I'm saying."

Sam looked at the clock on the dash. "Doubt he's at the office. It's long after hours."

"I've got his cell."

Sam glanced at the time again. "You have a phone?"

"No, threw it out before I left home."

"Good thinking."

Fool smiled—at least he did one thing right.

"You ever use a pay phone?"

"A what? Like they used in black and white movies?"

"You're cooking."

"Nah, thought they were long gone."

"They are but there is one up the road a bit. It's still good."

Fool was about to ask how Sam knew, but it didn't matter. The dude was full of surprises.

Sam eased the car onto the highway. The Mercedes was smooth but didn't have the same giddy-up as the Jag. That was still a question in Fool's mind. "Sam?"

"Yeah, boychik."

"The Jag. What…

"In due time. Right now, the priority is to get you to that phone. It's a few more miles."

Chapter Thirty-One

Something tickled Jasmine's face. She heard the plop water makes and smelled wet dirt. Her head didn't make sense of any of it. She was in sleep's clutch wandering in an unknown scene. She fought to stay there but a force jabbed at her. Pain, sharp but sporadic, invaded her being. The intensity of it grew until she couldn't bear it and woke with a scream. She tasted blood when her tongue swept her lips, and dirt. Her arm and hand refused to move to wipe her mouth. A sensation like hot coals swept through her shoulder. What the hell happened? Her heart pounded. She gulped air, frustrated by the throbbing, and panicked that death was about to swallow her. "No," she heard herself say, "not yet. I gotta live. Jesus, help me. Please… please." Tears trickled down her temples and she whimpered lying on the ground, not knowing or remembering how she got there. Her mind wandered. The aching drifted into an unconsciousness she more than welcomed.

A light caught her eye. It pierced the blackness. Instead of blood and dirt she smelled something antiseptic. She ran her tongue across her lips. The blood and grime—gone. She heard the steady hum of a machine and an occasional beep. She opened her eyes. She was in a room. She saw the outline of someone by the door.

* * *

"Hey, Doc, what's the story with the patient?" Officer Dietrich of the 4th Police District moved away from the doorway of room 2604 at U. of C. hospital.

Dr. S. Katzir, a middle-aged dark-haired woman, continued to look at a chart. "She's regaining consciousness. She came in with a list of injuries including broken ribs, a dislocated shoulder, and bullet wound."

"We didn't find an ID on her. Can I talk to her?"

The doctor glanced up. "You can try. I'm sure she's groggy."

Dietrich gave her a thumbs-up and went down the hall and into the room. He was aware she'd been brought in by ambulance along with a male/black who was D.O.A. Fingerprints of the dead victim identified him as Tysus Williams, aka Short Stuff or Shorty. His rap sheet indicated he had gang affiliation. A weapon was found at the scene in close proximity to the woman now lying in the hospital bed. Dietrich wanted to talk to her before he had the gun report. At this point he didn't need to advise her of Miranda warnings. He walked over to her bed.

"I'm Officer Dietrich, Chicago police department, can you tell me your name." He watched her eyes. They didn't focus. "Can you hear me?"

She made a gurgling sound.

"Are you all, right?"

Her face paled, then she retched.

"Nurse!" Dietrich ran out into the hallway calling for help. He stood outside the room as Dr. Katzir, and another medical assistant rushed in. Several minutes later a cleaning crew entered.

Dietrich moved down the hall a bit. He had a visceral reaction to someone vomiting. His stomach clutched and he broke into a sweat. He didn't understand it, given he'd seen a lot of gore and depravity in his job. Maybe it was loss of control that got to him.

Dr. Katzir found him pacing in front of a bank of elevators. "Didn't get too far, did you." She hid her smile. "It will take a few hours for all the anesthetic and shock to wear off. She's been through a lot of trauma."

Dietrich checked his watch. "Good to know, but there's a homicide and I need her awake. I don't have all day."

She shrugged. "Can't make her go faster. Nature will take its course."

"You…you don't understand. She's not under arrest. She can walk out of here."

"You have a problem, officer, but there's nothing I can medically do to help."

Dietrich's shoulders slumped. It was an argument he couldn't win.

"If it's any consolation, I don't think the patient is in any shape to go anywhere. If you have to leave, she'll still be there when you return."

"Well, that's something, Doc. Hope you're right."

Chapter Thirty-Two

J.P. glanced up from his desk and watched Simone strut the distance between his entry door and the chairs across from his desk. She took a seat in one of them. Everything about her—the dress, her hair—was immaculate. The blouse under her sport jacket was opened enough to reveal a glimpse of her breasts but not enough to be lewd. He easily recognized her perfume: the same from last night. This was not a woman on her way to or from the gym. Was she here to apologize or at the least…explain? He let her settle in her seat before delving into the topic on his mind.

"I didn't expect to see you," J.P. kept his voice calm. "Nice surprise. Coffee? A soft drink?"

"No thank you. Had some this morning."

J.P. folded his hands on the desk. He waited a few seconds as the awkwardness grew. He cleared his throat. "I'm amazed you're here, considering how last night ended." He focused on her. "I thought we…"

She sat back. "That's why I'm here. The evening surprised me too."

"Oh?"

"I didn't…didn't…" She began to tear. "I'm sorry." She reached into her portfolio-size bag and took a tissue. "I'm trying to be adultlike about this."

"About…? I'm confused. What are you crying about?"

She dabbed her eyes, then leaned forward. Her voice husky. "You hurt me, J.P."

"I…what? How? What did I do?"

"I invited you to my house because of your stated interest in architecture and the historical nature of the place. I thought you were a gentleman who wouldn't take advantage…"

"What the hell?"

"Let me finish, please."

J.P. stood.

"Sit, J.P., you're intimidating me."

J.P. stared at her for a few seconds, then resumed his seat. "Say whatever you want." He grabbed his ballpoint pen from the desk clicking its top.

"Please, J.P., would you stop that. This is as difficult to say as it may be to hear, but I must tell you."

He gave the pen one more click. "Okay… I'm listening."

Simone straightened her shoulders and sniffed the air. "Like I said, J.P., I had no idea inviting you to my house would lead to…" she swallowed hard, "to…" Her eyes misted again, "Sex. You tore my clothes– my beloved silk blouse, my panties." Her jaw trembled slightly. She looked at him, her eyes wide. "How…how could you?" She buried her face in her hands, then retrieved another tissue. "You bruised me. I have an appointment with my doctor later this afternoon."

J.P. didn't stir as she wove this fantastical story. If the bitch wasn't serious, he would have laughed her out of the office. *Tore her clothes…bullshit.*

"You know the worst thing, J.P.?" She didn't wait for his answer. "You didn't even bother to use a condom. I told you, no… pleaded, but you didn't listen. I warned you about coming inside of me, but you took no regard. Pregnancy is obviously not your concern." She paused, her hands shook, as she went into her purse and produced a document, dropping it in front of him.

Her voice changed to concern. "I realize what this could mean to your reputation, and I really don't want to hurt you like you hurt me. I'm not that kind of person. I think this matter can be resolved in an adult manner."

J.P. scanned the first page and rapidly turned to the next. When he concluded, he pushed the document slightly toward her. He cocked his head. "So, all you want is a mere one-seventy-five K to forget this incident. If I read this right."

She dabbed her eyes again and sniffed. "I'll never forget what you did to me last night. I'm letting you off cheap. A few dollars and you have a future, unlike me. I'm condemned to relive your brutality for the rest of my life."

J.P. licked his lips. "Did you write this proposal?"

"Most of it. I had some advice."

He raised his eyebrows. He wanted to punch the shit out of her, but he didn't. He hit the intercom button. "Tasha, would you come in and show Ms. Jenwick out." He leaned back.

"You're not going to agree?" Simone rose as Tasha entered.

"I'll think about it."

"Don't think too long. It would break my heart if we couldn't resolve this. You have until five p.m. today."

Chapter Thirty-Three

Fool stared into the darkness as Sam accelerated. Wherever Sam was taking him, it was beyond even the sticks. City lights and outlines of buildings disappeared. An occasional set of oncoming headlights passed, swallowed by the darkness.

"We'll be there in no time. This baby can move." Sam patted the steering wheel. "I love the open road."

"How fast you going?"

"Oh…about a hundred. Don't feel it though."

"S-h-i-t. Don't you worry about cops?"

"Out here? Nah. Probably there isn't one for God knows."

Fool let that thought settle. A few more miles went by when something caught his eye, and he checked the side-view mirror. "Well, there's something com'n behind you flashing red."

Sam glanced at his rearview. "I'll be. Could be an ambulance."

"You think? Any hospitals out this way?"

"I got this, boychik. Keep your mouth shut."

Fool glanced again and saw the lights getting larger. "Yeah, sure. You do the talkin'" His fingernails pressed into his palm. Jesus, he was done for. Damn Sam and whatever it was he was into. It was over. He'd never see his old lady again. What a fool he was.

Sam slowed to a stop. The other car pulled behind the Mercedes and aimed its spotlight.

"Get out of the car with your hands over your head," a male voice commanded through his vehicle's loudspeaker.

"Oh shit, Sam, you've done it now. God damn you."

"Nice. Now's not the time. Do what they say."

They got out of the Mercedes and stood by their respective doors. Two officers approached—one female the other male. Each had a hand on the weapon on their hip. The male approached Sam while examining the vehicle. He touched the rear taillight.

"You know how fast you were going?"

Sam nodded. "I do. The Mercedes Benz company asked me to test drive it. See what it can do under various conditions. I chose this road because it's lightly traveled at this time of night."

"Uh-huh. Your license and registration and do it slowly."

"They're in the car. May I get it?"

The officer glanced over at his partner who nodded. "Okay, yeah, go ahead." The officer held a high beam flashlight in his other hand and lit up the front area of the car.

Sam momentarily disappeared inside. Fool saw Sam rummage in the front console and hold up papers. He then got out. "Here you go. I also have a letter from Mercedes with my instructions."

The trooper did a quick check of the license and letter. "Stay where you are. Don't move. That goes for the kid, too. I'm going to my squad to check it out."

Sam turned to the female as soon as her partner walked away. "I must have made your night as I'm sure you don't get a lot of traffic."

She stood toward the rear passenger door of the Mercedes, several feet from David.

"You'd be surprised. The road isn't as deserted as you think."

"Is that so. I've been on it at all hours and never saw many cars. I certainly never saw police."

"It's your lucky night."

"Guess so. It goes without saying I would never have used it as a test for the vehicle if I thought it would endanger..."

"Save it for my partner. I'm here for the ride."

"Only pointing out what I thought was obvious."

The female officer stole a glance at her partner still in the police car.

Sam looked in the same direction. "Computers. Can't live with them or without them. Would it be all right for me and my nephew to put our arms down? Hands above our heads are not a position we're used to."

She nodded. "Yeah, guess so. You don't appear stupid enough to attempt to get away."

The interior light of the male's police car flicked on as he stepped out and walked toward Sam.

"Here you go, Mr. Lanier. Everything seems in order. I'm giving you a warning. Don't speed like that again." He tilted his head toward the vehicle. "At least not on this road." He turned to David. "Watch your old man. He seems to have a lead foot. Not a good example."

Fool half smiled. "Will do." He quickly climbed back into the passenger seat.

"Thank you, officers I'll watch it from now on." Sam waved and got into the Mercedes. He pushed the start button and gently eased onto the road. He eyed the rearview mirror as he gained distance.

Fool also checked the outside mirror. When he figured they weren't being followed, he turned to Sam. "Lanier? Your last name is Lanier spelled L-a-n-i-e-r? What the fuck?"

Chapter Thirty-Four

Big decided to head to his crib after leaving Jasmine and Shorty as roadkill on a deserted street. What ate at him was having his windshield cracked and the mess Jasmine made in his ride. He found blood spots on the steering wheel and on the passenger seat. The bitch didn't have the good sense to bleed out on the street. She had no respect. He made the right decision to get rid of her. She was trouble. As for Shorty, well, he was loyal like a puppy at feeding time. He'd miss him, but what was done was done...couldn't be helped.

Big was the boss man. He made decisions and didn't wimp from them. He'd have to tell the others somethin', especially since they liked having pussy that was easy and available. He dug into his pocket for a joint and lit it off the car's lighter. There will be other Jasmines. Show a bitch a few dollars along with stuff that made them feel so good, toss in some shiny shit, and they more than willing to spread their legs to keep his crew happy. *It's the way of the world.*

Big flipped on the radio. He typically didn't listen to the news. He'd play his music, but he might as well hear if somethin' was up. Some asshole talked about the Dow Jones, then gave local 411 about the shooting of the two bitches outside Fool's digs. He drew deeply on the joint. One was dead, the other still kick'n. He exhaled slowly and wondered which one—not that it mattered all that much in the scheme of things. Fool would get the message to stay the fuck away, no matter who remained breath'n. The hood was closed to him, that for sure.

Big grunted as he ran down the day's happenings. Getting rid of Fool solved a few things. Ain't goin' to be no trial if the Man don't have Fool. The joint was making him feel like a Sunday stroll in the park. He ticked off another. Not only won't Fool be stickin' his white dick into black pussy, he won't be in nobody's business...Big's or his crew. Big be the man, now—the only man. No more look'n at the white boy for his two cents' worth of shit. Big be the only voice to matter.

Big stepped on the gas and the Caddy giddy-upped, hitting sixty in seconds. It felt good, like he held all the power in the world. He flew by several cars, leaving them in his dust. He got a laugh out of that. He was hummin'. *Hmm this baby can sure move.* He patted the steering wheel. *Got to get you fixed and cleaned. Be respectable again.* He checked the rearview, then the speedometer. He needed to slow down. Didn't want to attract attention from the wrong kind…cops.

* * *

Anne opened her eyes. A man dressed in blue scrubs stood by her bed.

"I'm Dr. Hansen. You were brought here by ambulance. Do you know why?"

Anne coughed and pointed toward the jug of water.

"Oh, sure." Dr. Hansen poured a cup. "Don't rush."

A jolt of pain accompanied her effort to sit up. She blinked back tears as she reached for the water. Her hand trembled when she brought it to her lips. She could only drink it slowly. She had no other speed. The exercise exhausted her, and she fell back on her pillow. "Oh my God," she stammered, "what…" Her voice trailed off. Her heart raced and she stared vacantly into space. She heard bells. Her eyes closed. In a trick of time, she heard and felt nothing at all.

Charise. *I don't understand. Get up. You can't sleep in front of the house. Get up. The neighbors for God's sake, woman. David will be here…Jasmine? Thank God you're okay. What? I can't… Who's that… a firecracker…Why? A river flowing. A red river. Charise you should see… Charise? Help me…please God, help me.*

Chapter Thirty-Five

J.P. remained standing while Tasha showed Simone out. *Blackmail! She…she. Hell! I'm an attorney. A lawyer who can spot a snake from a distance. How could I have let this happen?*

He never considered himself reckless. A bit carefree but not stupid, even when it came to pussy. A lady's man but not a hound. There was a difference.

It took decades to build his practice. There were a handful of pissed-off clients, a few complaints to the ARDC (Attorney Registration and Disciplinary Commission), which were promptly dismissed.

He refocused his attention to Simone's document. He flipped the pages, reading quickly. "Son-of-a-bitch." He hunched over his desk, rekindling his anger at the outrageous lies and damages she sought. When he looked up, Tasha was leaning against his door.

"What was that about?" Her hands were folded across her chest.

"If I told you, you wouldn't believe it."

"Come on, J.P., I've been here long enough and seen a lot of weird shit. So, what was it?"

J.P. worked his facial muscles. He was fired up. "It had to do with last night…" He took a deep breath, then slapped the papers on his desk. "No, I shouldn't. I don't want you involved. You could become a witness. Give me a minute. You don't need this crap."

"Uh-huh." Her eyes blazed. "I think I know where you're goin'. I'm a big girl. Been with you when you had a tiny office. You've blessed me with a living—a good living. If I can help, let me. Just say thank you."

J.P.'s eyes teared. "This is not a good look." He used his handkerchief. "I appreciate that, Tasha." He paused. "I have an idea. Get a camera or your iPhone. Wait, you can use mine." He handed it to her. He began to unbutton his shirt but stopped after two. "Nope, bad choice. I'm not thinking so good." He refastened, then tucked in his shirt. "Call my doctor. Tell him I have to see him, immediately. If

Simone can pull this shit, so can I."

"You sure? I know how to take pictures."

"I'm sure you do but having my doctor do it puts it into a different realm. God knows what diseases or…" He waved his arms. "…I got from her." He stood and reached around to the small of his back. "For the record, it's killing me. Don't know what Simone did, but movement is a pain."

He shooed Tasha out of the office, his voice trailing after her. "Let me know when the doc can fit me in. You hear?" He resumed his seat at his desk and tossed Simone's agreement to a corner. He had work to do. He should call about Anne and certainly patch up things with Nora. Jesus, he better make it right with her. She could be his ace in the hole if this Simone shit gets way out of hand. He punched the intercom. "Tash, grab your pen."

"Okay, got it."

"Send a dozen roses to Nora."

"All right. You want a card or somethin'?"

"Yeah, good idea. I want it to say, 'working my way back. Dinner—your choice where…J.P.'."

He could imagine Tasha's reaction. "I know what you're think'n but I've got it under control. You've got to lay out the honey for the bee to come."

"That's fine by me, whatever you do, J.P.… only don't get stung."

* * *

Simone left J.P.'s office. Her high-heel shoes clicked on the marble floor until she reached the bank of elevators. She pushed the call button and waited. She tried to tamp down her smile but couldn't help herself. The shocked look on men, after being told that carnality costs, proved a constant amazement. Men thought sex was all inclusive in an evening…like airfare and a hotel. They pay for a meal, the booze, and in gratitude women naturally fall into bed.

She took a small makeup mirror and a lipstick applicator from her purse and used it. When she was done, she smacked her lips and returned the items to her purse. *The poor dears*, she thought, *after they've been informed, they grab their only meaningful parts*…as if she'd kicked them in the balls.

The elevator bell announced its arrival. She got in and pressed the button for the lobby. Her office was in another wing of the building with a different set of elevators.

She closed her eyes for a few seconds and recalled the disbelief on J.P.'s face. It was priceless. She strategized there was a high probability he'd crumble; after all, his reputation, legal and otherwise, was at stake. Such a pity. She calculated the cost of his several minutes of what he thought was joy. She took a deep breath. It was exorbitant, but then, that's what made those moments…precious.

The elevator door opened to the main floor. She checked her Piaget wristwatch. Her medical appointment was in forty-five minutes. Why return to the office on such a great day?

Her doctor's office was in the Water Tower Place and the stores she frequented were in the vicinity. Nothing could be easier. She could walk it, but…no, she must take care of herself. She had just suffered trauma and stress. Her physician needed to be convinced of that.

She stepped outside her building and walked to the curb to hail a cab. No Uber or whatever for her. She stuck her arm out and struck a pose showing just enough leg. Voilà… a yellow cab stopped. She climbed in and told him her destination. Cash was still king. There would be no record of this transaction.

She was giddy as the cab made a uey to go north on LaSalle. Business first, then a bit of pleasure.

Chapter Thirty-Six

"When were you going to tell me, Sam?" Fool was pissed. "You know what I think? You weren't. Nope, you were going to keep your last name all to yourself." Fool felt his face getting hot. He didn't wait for Sam to respond.

"Hell, we've been driving for over forty-five minutes and I ain't seen any phone booth. Just pitch black and nothingness. I should've told those cops you were kidnapping me. Mercedes Benz employee, my ass. You stole this car like you did the Jag."

Sam took his eyes off the road for a second or two and looked at Fool. "Didn't steal the Jag or this one. If you must know, I repo cars, then sell them. I was at the casino for a whole other purpose. Bumping into you was pure happenstance."

"Yeah? You can mouth your way out of anything. I'd almost believe you."

"Suit yourself. See the bluish light on your right…in the distance?"

Fool stared into the darkness. "Where?"

"We're coming up on it." Sam pointed.

"I'll be damned."

Sam pulled the car off the road and stopped. "Okay boychik, make the call."

Fool opened the door and had one foot on the gravel emergency lane. "What do I do? Never used this shit before."

"You have any quarters?"

"Quart…what?"

Sam reached into his pocket. "Here's some change. Drop it in the slot, then dial."

Fool took the money, not quite believing any of it would work. He stepped out of the car and walked over to the pay phone, kicking up dust. The headlights of the Benz lit the way. He stood in front of the damn thing and stared at it. Never seen one before except in an old movie. He looked back at the car for a moment, then gave the gizmo a hard stare. *Looks like a plain old phone, shit, nothin' to it.* He picked up the receiver and dialed J.P.'s cell number. There was no connection, shit, there was nothing at all. "Hello? Hello, J.P.?" He gripped the receiver harder—still nothing. He held it away from his face and gave it the once-over. *What the hell?*

"Boychik."

Fool dropped the phone. "What the… You scared the shit out of me. Never heard you coming."

"Sorry. I saw you standing there. Seemed like you were lost. You have to drop the quarter in the slot, dial the number, and the operator will tell you how much more you need."

Fool straightened. "I…I knew that. Nothin' for free. Thought I had to dial first. Anyway, I got it."

"Okay, I'll go back to the car."

Fool watched Sam get into the Benz before trying again. *Okay, I'll put the quarter in.* Then he grabbed the dangling receiver, heard the dial tone, and punched in J.P.'s number. Sure, enough an operator came on the line and told him it would be two dollars for the first three minutes. He stuffed all the quarters he had into the slot, and seconds later the call went through. After several rings, J.P.'s voice mail came on instructing the caller to leave a message. Fool made a split-second decision. He couldn't ask J.P. to call him back, and he certainly didn't want to leave his location. He hung up. He rested his hand on the receiver, debating whether he did the right thing. The clatter of the coins falling into the phone box shook him out of his reverie. He was no closer to finding out about his old lady than he was hours ago. Only now he was…a hell of a long way from Chicago hangin' with a crazy-ass dude. He kicked the dirt under his shoes.

Sam stood by his open car door. "So?"

Fool shuffled back to the Benz. "Ain't nothin'. J.P. didn't pick up and I didn't leave a message. What for? I ain't got no phone."

"Smart. No sense giving away your position when it would do you no good."

"Yeah, yeah. What happens now?"

"We get some rest and figure something in the morning."

Fool slung himself into the passenger seat. He stared, not focusing on much of anything. "You're the answer man. Where are we goin' to crash?" He scanned the blackness. "Ain't no hotel, motel, or house in sight."

"Don't you worry, boychik. I know these parts. There is light after darkness. Shut the door. We'll be fine."

Fool glared at Sam slinking down in his seat. "You the man, Sam. You know everything. I can't do shit now except hope my old lady is still breathing."

Sam reached over and patted Fool's hand. "We can both pray on that."

* * *

Jasmine struggled to sit up. She was hooked up to so many tubes and machines. One thing for sure, her shoulder hurt like hell swathed in layers of bandages. Somewhere on her bed or side table was a call button, but it was playing hide and seek. She gave up, after what seemed like five minutes of looking…exhausted. She fell back on the pillow. "Yo nurse." Her voice cracked. Her whisper didn't carry. She tried again. It wasn't going to happen. She was wide eyed, staring at the ceiling. Her mouth drier than a desert, not that she had ever been in one. Water. If only she could get…water. Her whole being focused on this one task. Succeeding would make everything right. She took a few breaths, ignoring the sharp pain every time she inhaled. She told herself at the count of ten, she'd sit up. At seven she girded herself—eight, nine, ten. *All right bitch, do it.* She rose slowly…breathing like a son-of-a-gun. Her movement caused one of the machines to ding, then another. A nurse appeared in the doorway.

"Everything all right?"

A smile touched Jasmine's face or was it more of a grimace. She pointed to the pitcher on the side table.

"Oh sure, baby. Let me help you. I'm Evelyn." She stepped in and poured Jasmine a cup. "Drink it slow, otherwise you'll throw it up."

Jasmine used her eyes to thank her. Evelyn placed a straw in Jasmine's mouth.

"Baby, I've been here a long time and seen a lot. You got shot in the shoulder."

"I did?"

"Uh-huh.

"Is that why I'm in pain when I breathe?"

"You also broke a couple of ribs."

Jasmine touched her side and winced.

"Child, you looked as if you've been through a war or somethin' when the ambulance brought you. What happened?"

Chapter Thirty-Seven

Big could smell a problem before it smacked him upside his head. The minute he drove into the oversize garage next to his crib, his homies, Leon, Maurice, and Trè, sauntered to his whip, scowls on their faces. *What the fuck?* He had to deal with these fools, after all he'd been through? On top of that, his pride and joy Caddy damaged and dirtied up by that bitch.

The three of them gathered around the driver's door. Didn't give Big much room to get out.

He rolled the window a crack. "Hey, I'm try'n to open the damn door. Move. What's wrong with y'all."

"We heard the news, Big." Trè acted as the spokesman. "Shorty laid out along with the bitch."

Big took the flash and digested it. "Shorty shot? Jasmine? You sure you heard right?" He furled his brow. His eyes narrowed. "Hmm. No way. I left Shorty with the bitch. He's fucking her brains out." He looked over the crew and grunted. "I got to get business done. Get out of my way."

All three shook their heads but moved slightly back. "Not the word on the street," Leon volunteered.

Maurice stepped toward the front of the Caddy. "Your front window busted."

Big turned slightly in Maurice's direction. "Uh-huh. Some asshole threw a rock from an overpass. I'm lucky I wasn't killed."

Maurice examined the damage, then walked toward the driver's door. "Don't look like no rock to me."

Big had one foot on the garage floor. He used the steering wheel for leverage to push the rest of him out. "I say a rock did that, Maurice. You call'n me a liar?" Big rose to his full girth.

Maurice skirted looking at Big. "No sir. Don't mean to disrespect."

"That's better." Big relaxed.

"Or it could 'a been somethin' else," he said in a loud enough whisper.

Big leaned on his door. "I don't like your attitude, Maurice." He slid his hand to his side to grip his Glock. *Oh shit.* He planted it next to Jasmine as she was dying. He better think of somethin'.

"Can't deal with your nonsense. Shorty laid out…shit. He was doin' pretty good the last I saw him. I got things to do. Get out of my way."

Big stepped a few feet away from the Caddie, eyeing the three of them. Which one had balls? "Hmm." Not much there, he concluded. He was the one who got them the wheels, so they could drive like shit, layin' rubber and laugh'n their asses off. They all got respect work'n the hood for him…pussy, drugs, and green. What more did they want? No one had moved. Big cleared his throat.

"You fuckers deaf? Where the hell you pick up such crap?"

Leon stared at his shoes. Maurice rubbed his chin. He opened his mouth…no words. Trè looked past Big.

"The street say you messed up."

"Come again?"

"You heard me the first time. You capped Shorty and the bitch too."

"What you say?" Big shook his head and laughed. "That's crazy. You've been smoke'n too much weed. You out of your mind. Why would I want to put Shorty down? We grew together." Big let his question settle. He backed up a little more. "Shorty was as much part of this crew as y'all. Nah, no way."

The three kept staring.

Big rested his hand by his gun side pretending the Glock was there. He rubbed his chin with his other hand and grunted. "Y'all getting' me pissed and y'all know you don't want to do that. I sees where you goin', so I'll hold up. As you boys are feel'n so poorly, I was going to wait but…I'll tell you straight. Part of the bennies work'n for me was the ho. She was yours. The girl each of you fucked got a change of mind…. didn't want to put out anymore. Said she was tired and a little sore from all the action and wanted out." A few smiles crept on their faces.

"Ol Jasmine… the bitch liked it." Leon licked his lips.

"She did. Ain't no lie," Big agreed. "I didn't want to tell you until I lined up a few replacements. But Shorty thought she was joking and went for her. They got into a tussle in the back seat. I warned them to cut the crap. I was slowing down when they jumped out. I hit the brakes so hard the air bags exploded. Next thing I hear is pow, pow, pow. The damn ho pumped Shorty and Shorty did her. No idea the little bitch was packin'. I swear. Nothin' I could do but get the hell out of there." Big put out a large toothy smile. "Shorty was like a brother to me. I'd never cap him."

All three of them listened like Big was a preacher and they in church. Big held their gaze waiting for the amen but it never came. Out of the corner of Big's eye he saw Trè shaking from side to side like he was Stevie Wonder. He watched the other two catching a glimpse. Big got the message. Trè was the one with the balls. "What the fuck the matter with y'all. I told what happened. Now there's business to do. Get."

"Ain't what happened, Big." Trè let the words out slowly. "Ain't the way it went down."

Big put his arm out, signaling to Trè he should shut his mouth. "How the fuck do you know. You weren't there. I say it's exactly how it went."

"You are lyin'," the three said as if they were a choir. Trè then led. "Someone saw you…eyed the whole thing. You shot Shorty in the head, not the ho. The street don't lie." Trè ran his hand over the Caddie's hood as the other two closed in. "She sure is fine, Big, even with the smashed window."

Big never in his life thought about the length of a second. He never thought about minutes or the meaning of life. He watched, his mouth gaping as his three homies pulled out their pieces. In that fraction of time, all he could think of was their betrayal. They were going to shoot him like a damn dog. *What goes around, comes around* was his final thought. Three shots.

Chapter Thirty-Eight

Fool opened his eyes, looking over his bed. Where was he? *Never slept in such a large one. Didn't know a bed could be that big.* Jasmine popped into his head. M-a-n he could be fuck'n two Jasmines and there would be enough room for a third. *Cool thought.*

He threw the sheet and cover away, sat, then scratched his head. He zeroed in on the black and white striped wallpaper that lined one wall. It was r-e-a-l fancy-like. Wasn't torn like the ones he was used to seeing. The lamp next to his bed even had a lamp shade that wasn't moth-eaten. He nodded and stretched. *Sure, as hell beats a jail cell.*

"Breakfast?"

Fool looked over.

Sam stood in the doorway. "Did you get a good night's sleep?"

"Uh-yeah." Fool rubbed his eyes. "What is this place? Where am I; and what are you doing with an apron around your waist?"

Sam glanced down. "I'm cooking."

Fool sniffed the air. "Smells good."

"Glad you approve. The shower is down the hall, and fresh towels are in that dresser." He pointed.

"I'll get my ass moving."

Fool stood naked studying the dials to the shower. *Never seen anything like it.* He pressed a button on the wall and lights danced around what he thought was the shower head. He tried another and spray came from all directions. He bent over to protect himself. "Cut that out. D-a-m-n. Like a bitch in heat." He fumbled around the switches until he found the one that made the water come straight down like it was supposed to. He didn't waste time with much soap. He rinsed, dried off, and got dressed. He smelled Sam's cooking and hurried out the bathroom and down the long-ass staircase.

The kitchen could fit an apartment and a half. Fool knew what an oven and stove looked like, but nothing like this. Each had their own counter. Each had dials, switches…Jesus, just to cook some Goddamn eggs and what he thought was bacon. Sam opened the fridge to get a carton of juice. Holy shit, the whole Jewel store could fit in the damn thing.

"Sit." Sam pointed to a well-cushioned chair next to a large round table.

"I don't believe what I'm see'n. Is this some sort of castle? Hollywood Mansion? Whatcha got goin', Sam?"

"You like eggs with onions, tomatoes, mushrooms, and salami?"

"I…I…sure. You're not answer'n."

"You have to get the onions right…golden brown. Mess the onions and the rest wouldn't be worth eating." Sam shifted the fry pan and stirred the contents.

Fool shifted in his seat. "Okay, if you don't want to tell me. Fine. Give me whatever and I'll be going. Nice to have met you, Mr. Sam Lanier."

Sam looked over, shrugged, and returned to cooking. "Coffee will be done in a minute."

"You are something else. You work for CIA? FBI? You don't say nothin' you don't want to. Got to respect that. You make a hell of a secret agent—some kind of George Smiley."

Sam looked up from the fry pan. "You know of John le Carré? Good taste, boychik."

Sam continued cooking. Damn, the smells made Fool's mouth water.

"All right—done."

* * *

Officer Dietrich returned to U. of C. hospital. The lab results were in, and Jasmine's fingerprints were all over the Glock. Time to take her into custody, then call the State's Attorney's office for final approval of homicide charges.

He passed the nurse's control desk searching for Dr. Katzir. She wasn't there. He checked his watch…4 p.m. The place was unusually quiet. Must be shift change. He grabbed his pad out of his pocket and flipped to the page where he had scribbled 2604. He checked the numbers as he walked down the corridor. They were odd beginning with 2601. He must have made a wrong turn or something. He glanced around, but all the corridors looked alike. *Where the hell are the evens?* He stopped and backtracked. He walked around the control console and took a different route that angled off from where he had been. Sure, enough the digits next to the rooms were even starting with 2620. He recalled Jasmine's was next to last near the sign for the elevator. He didn't bother to knock on the closed door. He twisted the doorknob and entered. The bed was empty. "Hmm." He calmed himself with the thought she may be having tests…X-rays, MRI's, not so out of the ordinary. He tried the bathroom. No one. He did another take of the vacant bed. The machines with their attachments were unplugged chirping and beeping. Now that's unusual. Did staff notice? Respond? He felt a lump in his throat. His hands grew cold even though he could hear his heart pound. *Damn, I should never have left.* He exited the room and hurried toward the nurse's station.

"Anyone here? Hello? Dr. Katzir?" The whole floor couldn't be empty. He raised his voice.

"Yes? Can I help you? Sir, keep your voice down. There are patients here." She came out from a room two doors from the nurse's station.

"Officer Dietrich, Chicago Police." He held his wallet with his badge for her to see. "Is Dr. Katzir around? She was attending a female in room 2604."

"Katzir? Let me check." She took a seat behind one of the computers and typed. Minutes ticked away like hours. "Ma'am?"

She, Ms. Elaine, looked up. Her eyes read *what the fuck,* but her tone stayed professional. "I'm looking her up. It'll be another minute or two."

He shifted from foot to foot—like a kid in need of a bathroom. *How much longer?*

Nurse Elaine interrupted his self-pity. "Dr. Katzir checked out an hour ago. She may, though, be in emergency. A few new cases arrived."

"What about the patient in 2604?"

"I need to see your identification again."

Dietrich grabbed at his pocket and retrieved his ID. "It hasn't changed from a few minutes ago."

"A few minutes ago, you asked about a doctor, not a patient. It's about security. Something you should know all about. Let me see your name and badge number again so I can record it."

Nurse Elaine went back to the computer, hands flying over the keyboard. "Okay, Officer Dietrich, I see the patient's name. She's in 2604."

"I know that. The room is empty."

"That's impossible." A thin smile covered her face as she attacked the information displayed on her screen. After several seconds, she glanced up. "According to the computer the patient is in room 2604."

Dietrich took a breath. "We're past that. She isn't there. Do you mind coming with me to the room?"

It was her turn to draw a deep breath. "The computer..." She glanced at the screen, then looked at Dietrich. "All right, officer, let's go."

The various machines were still chirping when they entered Jasmine's room.

"Oh, this isn't right." Nurse Elaine went to one of the machines and pushed a button, ending the noise. "The patient should be here. I wonder where..."

Dietrich scanned the room again. "Are they doing any tests on her?"

Elaine shook her head. "Not mentioned in the computer. Where could she be?"

"Gone, I'd say. She's gone."

Chapter Thirty-Nine

Simone sat in her doctor's spacious waiting room. It was more like an airport gate lounge. Her childhood memory of such places was nothing like this. Gone were the magazines, whether outdated or not, replaced by TV monitors in several locations. Nurses escorted would-be patients like flight attendants to their seats. The only thing missing was the offer of coffee, tea, or a soft beverage.

At first, after she checked in, it was fun watching the parade of people. Would she recognize anyone? Was that the weather person on channel 7 sitting near the front? Simone didn't want to stare. She couldn't decide and her interest soon frittered away, replaced by restlessness. She checked the clock on the wall as well as her Piaget wristwatch every few… According to her calculations, her doctor was late. She had been sitting for over ten minutes. This would not do. She was working up her complaint and resentment when her name was called. In that split second—all was forgiven.

Meghan, the doctor's assistant, led Simone into the inner sanctum. Once inside, they walked down two corridors and stopped outside examination room…forty-four.

"There's a blue gown to change into. You can leave your bra but everything else comes off. Dr. Stennis will be with you in a few minutes."

Meghan left before Simone could dare question. Obviously, the poor dear didn't know. Just as well. Simone found a chair and took a seat. This was less an examination and more of an explanation. Dr. Stennis had been to this rodeo a time or two before. It was always good to have an ally. Someone knowledgeable. Someone, who with the right amount of incentive, testified and wrote winning reports that resulted in big bucks. Simone checked the time again. It was nearing one thirty.

There was a polite knock on the door. Seconds later, Dr. Stennis came in. A woman in her mid-thirties-early-forties, her dark hair tied into a ponytail.

"How are you, Simone? I got your message." Dr. Stennis's gold necklace caught the light in the room.

Simone wrung her hands. "Not good." She shook her head. "Not good at all." Her eyes misted.

Dr. Stennis took Simone's hand in hers and leaned forward with concern. "What happened?" She held up her hand. "Wait, let's record it." She took her phone from her pocket and nodded.

"It was…" Simone's voice drifted off. "Terrible…just…please don't make me relive…" She began to sniffle and looked around for Kleenex.

The doctor retrieved a box from a desk drawer. "Here."

Simone dabbed her eyes and blew her nose. "Thank you." Her voice shook. "I…I should have…learned. I shoulda… He seemed to be so kind, caring… you know. I let him drive me home last night. As soon as we got inside…oh my G-d…every…things changed." She grabbed more Kleenex. "It was a nightmare…What he did…"

"Catch your breath."

Simone subtly opened her purse and deftly retrieved an envelope. "He's a lawyer," she sniffed, "big time." She glanced at the packet in her hand and let it fall onto Dr. Stennis's lap.

"What's his name?" Stennis placed her hand over the envelope and dropped it into her coat pocket.

"J.P. Wilson."

"I heard of him. Criminal law, if I remember right."

Simone blinked. "Yes, I think. I don't know. He talked about himself so much I stopped listening."

Stennis cleared her throat. "What happened once the two of you got into your house?"

Simone covered her eyes as if the room was spinning.

"Are you all right? You're as pale as a ghost."

Simone mumbled, "Water…I…faint."

Stennis reached for a paper cup and filled it. "Here. Drink slowly."

"Okay…" Simone's hands shook. She spilled a little taking a sip. She took another and she stopped trembling and relaxed. "Thanks. I think I'm better."

Stennis waited. "Are you up to continuing?"

Simone nodded.

"You're aware that after your examination, I will have to report this violence to the authorities."

Simone placed her hand by her mouth. "I must continue." She wiped her eyes with a tissue, "but do it first thing tomorrow. I'll call."

Chapter Forty

"They're beautiful, J.P., but don't think for a minute you're out of the doghouse."

"Nora, you got the flowers, great." J.P. stretched his legs on his desk, leaning back in his chair, the phone by his ear. "I know I screwed up last night, and I'm deeply sorry. Really."

"Uh-huh. Let's not go there." She sounded agitated.

"There's a second part to my peace offering. You can choose anyplace you'd like for dinner."

"O-k-a-y?" Silence followed.

"Nora?"

"J.P.... what...I mean the flowers are nice...beautiful, and dinner...well..."

"Nora, I acted horrible."

"You did but that's beside the point... damn it."

"Sorry...I..."

"Shut up, J.P. I'm trying to say something."

"Okay, okay..."

"You're doing this out of guilt; that's not what I want. None of it."

"I'm not."

She breathed into the phone. Her voice strained. "I'm not looking for... I mean...I know your reputation. I don't want to be an afterthought...one hot night and adios."

"You're not. That's not what this is about. I thought we had hit it off."

"I don't know...J.P. What you..."

"Nora, I'm serious. I was an ass. Should never have happened."

"You're smooth, J.P. Smooth. The words flow but I don't think... Forget it...just forget it. I don't want your pity. I'm a big girl. I've been around the block. I've been with guys like you and end up on the short end. Don't want to do it again. I've gotten pride in my old age. Don't want to deal with any more bullshit."

"Come on, Nora, give me a chance."

"I've heard that line too many times. Nope. J.P., take your flowers and..."

J.P. heard a loud click. "Nora?" He sat up and stared at his phone. *What the hell was going on?* Strike two and it was only the afternoon. He was at a loss to explain how a nice gesture could be so misinterpreted. *Am I clueless? Have things changed that much? When did that happen?* He drummed his fingers on his desk. He needed to get out of the office...clear his head. He checked the time, then asked Tasha over the intercom when his doctor's appointment was.

"In an hour."

He stood, grabbed his coat, and left his office. "Probably won't be back today," he told Tasha as he passed her desk heading for the door. "If there's time, I'll check on Anne at the hospital. Hopefully, I'll be able to talk with her."

"No problem. I'll hold down the fort. If something big happens, I'll call."

"You're always my man Friday." He stopped. "I mean my girl. Woman..."

"Get your ass out the door. Jesus." She shook her head and returned to her computer screen.

* * *

"So, what's bothering you?" Dr. Bergen ran down J.P.'s chart, sitting on a stool while his patient sat across from him. "I've warned you to ease up on the booze. It's going to screw you up."

"You're funny, Doc. I'm down to only two or three."

"A day or a week?"

"I'll let you know. But I'm not here for that. I need you to take a look at my back."

Bergen had a pair of those Chuck Shumer-type glasses perched on the tip of his nose. He peered through them, looking at J.P. "Why? What happened?"

J.P. unbuttoned, then removed his shirt. "Take a look."

Bergen slid over. "Did you have a fight with an alley cat?"

"Kind of. Although of the human variety."

"Whatever the two of you were doing, it seems she was into it." He took a pair of surgical gloves from a box on his desk and touched J.P.'s back.

He yelped. "That hurts."

"I'll put some antibiotic ointment on it."

"Before you do, can you take a photo."

"I don't under… J.P., what is this about?" The doctor's glasses didn't have much more to go before they fell off his face.

"What? Isn't that procedure?"

"Not usually. I document it, of course, but a photo?" He shook his head, then stroked his chin. He tapped J.P.'s shoulder and studied his back again. He lightly touched the area below the neck, then brushed J.P.'s scapular and interscapular regions. "Your alley cat has some very sharp claws. She did a number on your back. Luckily the scratches aren't very deep…just numerous." He slid over to face J.P. "For the record, whatever the two of you were doing was consensual?"

"Of course. I'd never… You've known me for too long to think… She was passionate, too passionate…"

"And now her claws are aimed at a different part of your anatomy?"

"You got it."

Chapter Forty-One

Fool dug into his eggs like a man who hadn't eaten in days. His fork stopped in mid-air after two mouthfuls. "Damn good shit, Sam, damn good. Never had salami and all this other crap in the same dish. Hell, you could start a Michelin three-star—you'd load up on coin."

Sam had taken a seat across the table. He peered over his coffee cup. "You keep surprising me. George Smiley, now this. What do you know about Michelin dining?"

"I know enough to say it. Saw it a few times on those TV cooking shows and school library."

"Library?"

"Yeah. It was cool. The bitches liked going there." A smile crossed his lips. "The librarian lady was half-blind and deaf. We did whatever we wanted. Scared the shit out of the woman most of the time. But every now and then I'd crack a book. One was about French women and food. It kept her happy and quiet. To go along you have to get along. Ain't that so, Sam."

"You're full of wisdom, this morning. More eggs?"

Fool eyed the bowl, then his plate. He still had room but wondered why Sam was stalling. Wasn't saying anything about Chicago and his old lady. He gave Sam a quick glance and decided to play it out. Why the hell not, the food was bitch'n. If anything, *Sam works on his own time.* Fool nodded. "Bring it on."

Sam gave him a generous portion.

Fool let the stuff rest a bit, then attacked. He stuffed his mouth and gulped it down. He had enough. Fool looked straight at Sam, who looked unconcerned...couldn't care less. "I want to let you know, food ain't go'n to shut me up. I thank you for it and I've taken my time but I still have an itch. You haven't answered anything I've asked this morning... last night. Nothing since we met." He cleared his throat. "I'm done and I'm getting the hell out. I like to know how and why my bread is buttered. Somewhere along the way a payment always comes due."

Sam took a bite from a toasted bagel and chased it with coffee. He put the cup down. "Where would you go and how?"

Fool laughed. "That's easy Sam, the Benz."

Sam roared. "The Benz? Boychik, it's gone...early this morning."

Fool dropped his fork. "Huh? I don't..." His stomach did somersaults. It took him a few seconds to get his thoughts together. "This is what I mean. I'm tired of the games. Didn't sign up for it. I need answers." He slapped the table. "I need to get to Chicago. My old lady may be dead. I don't have time to deal with your shit." He started to get up.

"Calm down, David. I told you I will help, and I will."

"Yeah?" Fool sat. "What's the plan, Jack?" He leaned over the table.

"First, you'll try your lawyer, again. If that doesn't work, we'll head back to Chicago."

"With what? You say you got rid of the Benz."

"True, but transportation isn't the issue. It's keeping you safe from the police and your other 'friends'."

Fool stared at Sam while contemplating his options. There weren't many. He really didn't know where he was exactly. So far Sam hadn't done anything crazy, at least to him. The digs were spectacular and the food, beyond complaint. If this was blackjack, Sam showed a king to his fourteen. Taking another card was a gamble. He'd go along until the time came.

* * *

Jasmine dozed after the nurse left—quite asleep or awake. Two men entered her room. She rubbed her eyes. "Y'all taking me for tests?" One nodded. She let out a sigh, relaxed, and began to drift. Sleep did not want to leave. Something, though, didn't seem right. Did the nurse say somethin' about more tests? She was in a haze, but she forced herself to stay awake.

Their dress seemed to be off. Orderlies had V-neck green or grayish/blue shirts with lettering; some, though, wore masks. Damn Covid. These men had their faces covered, dressed in black, and didn't say anything. The taller of the two stood beside her bed. The other began to yank the tubes connecting her with the various machines.

"Hey, what the fuck you doing? Yo, stop… Who are you? I'm calling…" She fumbled for the call button. One of the men knocked it away.

She struggled to sit up. Her legs kicked the sheet from her. Something was forced over her face and muffled her scream. She did the best she could to put up a fight, but it was over quickly. She lost her will, then consciousness.

She awoke and found herself chained to a wall, a dirty bed sheet covering her.

Chapter Forty-Two

Simone left her doctor's office secure in the knowledge that her battle plan was ready. The doctor not only heard her story but also used the rape kit tests and found the evidence needed in case J.P. denied he'd had sex with her. Men as a rule don't think too much ahead of their pleasure. If J.P. didn't agree to her demands, his life was about to become… She sighed and steeled herself for whatever may come. It was such a messy business.

She donned a pair of dark glasses, stepped outside the office building, and decided to shelve her earlier plan of shopping. With an eye on the forthcoming matter, it wouldn't play well; besides, the doctor stuff had changed her mood. Instead, she'd walk back on Michigan Avenue. A part of her wanted to be rid of who she had become. Lose herself in the crowd, free of cynicism, and look at the world with bright eyes. She was once… that. The world was a wonderment full of bright tomorrows—until it wasn't.

Love. She eyed a young couple, possibly late twenties/early thirties, holding hands as they strolled down the street. What the hell did they know what awaited them? She stopped at the corner for the traffic light. Did that seem harsh? Sometimes, it worked out. The light turned green. Nah, love settles into an ebb and flow of life. Eyes stray and the body follows. The sweetness lost in an array of excuses, rationalization, and hurt.

J.P. didn't bother with the handholding. She knew from the very moment he laid eyes on her at the health club what he wanted and what he was all about. Most men, though they thought themselves smooth and suave, were obvious.

How ironic he was representing Anne's son. Anne, wide-eyed once, so believing. Her wedding, an event of beauty. The words, spoken so eloquent and full of lasting promise. It was all so vivid that only a honking car saved Simone from being run over. Simone gave the driver the finger and continued her journey to her office. She hadn't thought of

Sol, Anne's husband, in a while. She and he had a good thing going. Despite being Anne's friend, Simone listened as Sol described to her a glorious future full of passion and travel to places like Paris, London, New York. It made putting up with Sol's foul-mouthed little gangbanger son bearable. Anne ran the business and didn't have time for much. It may have been her excuse, or she chose not to see.

Sol was needy. He'd do anything to keep their affair going. Playing him was so easy. Did she think of herself as immoral? She smiled. Not really...she liked him, at least in the beginning. The promises he made. He swore he'd leave Anne. "Nothing could keep us apart," he'd whisper into Simone's ear as they lay together, exhausted and content.

She was a bit naïve then, too. Weeks turned into months and then a year and then another and another. Time and changed circumstances made her grow up. Affairs, she realized, like anything else, cost.

The walking got Simone thirsty. She spotted a Starbucks a few doors down. Inside, the line was at a minimum and her latte order was handled quickly. She found a seat facing the window. She took a sip. The warmth felt good. She checked her phone for messages. A part of her hoped there was one from J.P., although he had several hours to go before five o'clock. She wasn't all that disappointed in not finding one.

The phone remained in her hand. Her mind wandered to Sol's last call to her. He told her he was parting with Anne the next day. He just omitted he was leaving everyone and everything. It was a monologue of things he should have done and things he wanted to do. He didn't apologize for the money and gifts he'd given her. Said she was worth it. Wished he had more, but now money was tight. Life had become too complicated. He suspected Anne had found out. Someone told.

Simone recalled his ironic laugh. "Nothing is forever," he'd said. He had racked his brain as to who was the traitor, but then they weren't all that careful.

Simone played with the rim of her coffee cup. That day when the little gangbanger found Sol hanging in the garage—Jesus. Simone felt her eyes water. All these years later and the memory tugged at her heart. That's what happens when emotions interfere.

She finished her coffee, then glanced at life outside the window.

* * *

Anne opened her eyes. She was startled by the machines attached to her, the beeping, the gurney/bed, what passed as clothes. Where was she? Her house. She was about to go into her home. A sensation like white heat shot through her and made her look at her bandages., She remembered. *Someone shot me. Damn the pain.* She looked wildly about, focusing on nothing. *Charise? Jasmine? Alive?* She drew her breath sharply. *What happened to them?* Concentrate. The ambulance. Sirens. She was in a hospital. She gazed across her bed and took in the opened door to her room. She saw a hallway and heard voices. She wanted to scream to catch their attention but didn't have the strength. She broke into a cold sweat. Her heart raced. Panic rose. *Call for help? There's a button somewhere...think.* She shifted focus to the contraptions hanging on the guardrails of the bed. She grabbed an oblong device full of buttons. She pushed them all. Seconds later a voice.

"Hello. Can I help you?"

The response startled Anne. She fumbled with the remote, then grabbed it and held it close to her mouth. "Eh, yes, yes you can. I need help."

"Are you in pain?"

"I—I—please, I—I—help. I...questions."

"Okay, we'll be there in a few minutes." The female voice sounded tired.

There were no clocks in the room and her watch wasn't on her arm. Another mystery. How long had she been here, in this room? Was it night? Morning? She concentrated on the hallway. She held the clicker thing tightly. More anxiety.

Another voice: this time it came from a middle-aged man wearing a blue coat. He stepped into her room and came toward her.

"I'm Dr. Hanson. I introduced myself a while ago, but you were still under the effects of sedation. How are you feeling?

"I...I'm not sure. What happened?"

He leaned closer. "You don't remember?"

"I do...sort of." She closed her eyes, then opened them and flinched. I...I got shot."

The doctor nodded. "Do you recall where you were?"

"My house. I was at my house. We drove there, Charise and I." She paused and swallowed hard. The doctor's gaze glued to her face.

"What happened then?"

"This is where it gets, I don't know..." She scratched her cheek. "Fuzzy. I...I turned; saw someone I knew...Jasmine, my son's girlfriend. I said.... something, I think—then shots."

"How many?"

"A bunch. At least three or four. I know I fell. Don't know what happened after that. Is Charise....Char...." Tears formed. "Was she...killed?" she whispered. Her hand gripped the edge of the sheet.

Doctor Hansen placed his hand over hers. "I don't know. She wasn't brought here."

"So, there may be a chance?"

He shrugged. "If you give me her full name and birth date, I'll try to run it down."

"Thanks." She wiped her face with her hand. "And Jasmine?"

"Give me the information and I'll see what I can do."

"Thank you.... thank you." Anne closed her eyes and said a prayer under her breath.

Chapter Forty-Three

Officer Dietrich and nurse Elaine stood by Jasmine's empty hospital room.

"I can't believe she's…she's gone, as you described, Officer. Things like that don't happen here." Nurse Elaine glanced into the room, then down the hallway.

"Uh-huh, then please illuminate. Why isn't she in her bed, and all the tubes are dangling?"

"I'm sure there's an explanation." She paused. "Someone must have forgotten to enter her location in the computer. I'm sure there's an update."

Dietrich rubbed his face. Time was wasting. "Then check the computer again."

They marched down the corridor to the nurse's station. Nurse Elaine grabbed a chair and attacked the keyboard. Dietrich couldn't view the monitor, but every few seconds Elaine typed furiously, then glanced at the screen and typed some more.

"Well?"

"I…I'm at a loss. I may have to call the police."

"I am the police, damn it. Are there cameras?"

"Please don't speak to me in that tone. Of course there are cameras."

"Good. Now, we're getting somewhere. How are they accessed?"

She hesitated. "I don't…probably call security or the administration."

"Do it."

Elaine squinted, then sighed. "I've never had to do this before. Just a minute." She reached into a drawer and retrieved a dog-eared loose-leaf book. She ran down a page, then another, and another.

Dietrich cleared his throat. After a few more seconds, he tapped his foot.

"I'm searching under Security/Cameras. I know you're impatient, Detective. I'm trying. There's everything but… wait a minute. I think I found the number. I have to put on my glasses."

"Glasses? I'll read it to you.

Elaine opened one drawer of the desk, then another.

Dietrich reached over to grab the book.

"Officer, you can't do that. It's against protocol. Now let go." She grabbed an end. "Please, you're wasting time." Some of the pages flew out of the binder. "See what you've done. Now I have to pick up all these and..."

Dietrich bent down and grabbed a handful. "Here." He leaned over her monitor. "There may be a murderer on the loose."

"Detective Dietrich I understand the severity of the circumstance. Please..."

He wanted to tear that book from her, but he controlled himself. Making more of a fuss wasn't going to get things better. He watched her put the pages back, then continue the search for her glasses, finding them in her purse. Using her finger to underline the number she dialed. He heard the dial tone. The phone rang and rang.

"No one answered." She hung up with a blank look on her face.

"Does the book indicate where their office is?"

"Oh, that's an idea. I'll look." She used her finger again to search the page. "Yes. Yes, it does. It's in the basement, Three South. Use elevator C."

Dietrich took off. There was elevator B and as he went farther along the hallway, elevator A. Somewhere along the corridor, he must have missed C. He broke into a small trot, backtracking, and found it close to Jasmine's vacated room. He punched the call button, but the damn thing had its own mind. Waiting, he searched the ceiling for security cameras. If they were there, they were discreetly hidden. Seconds that seemed like minutes passed until a bell rang announcing the car's arrival. The door opened slowly like an elderly person having difficulty walking. He stepped in and pressed B for basement. The door wheezed shut. Once closed, the car didn't move. It seemed to take time to process its new instruction before it shuddered and made its descent. Reaching the destination, another delay before Dietrich could finally step out. All he had to do now is find the security room... Three South. He figured there wouldn't be a large sign for it, so he walked, intently checking out the various nooks and crannies of the hospital's basement. For a solid five minutes he searched without success. He spotted a person several yards away wearing overalls and a work shirt.

"Hey, excuse me, can you help?"

The fella continued walking as if he didn't hear.

"Hey," Dietrich shouted.

The man stopped. "You talking to me?"

"Yeah." Dietrich went toward him. "I'm looking for the security office." He held out his badge. "Chicago Police."

The man scratched his head. "S-e-c-u-r-t-y office, down here?"

Dietrich was now a few feet from him. The name George was written on the man's shirt. "That's what the nurse upstairs told me."

"I don't know about that. Never seen it down here. Always been on the first floor next to 'Billing'."

"You sure about that?"

"At this place what you see today may not be there tomorrow, but that's where it was the last time I looked."

Dietrich checked his watch. Too much time had already passed. "Can you take me there? I don't want to get lost again."

"I was on my lunch break," he paused. "Aw hell…sure. We'll take elevator E. It's this way."

Dietrich's police radio chirped as he took a step. "Hold on." He motioned George to stop.

"Unit 4224?"

He held the radio to his ear. "Unit 4224, Dietrich."

"What's your location?"

"U. of C. Hospital."

"A young Black female in her twenties with bullet wounds was brought to U. of C. about fifteen minutes ago. Check it out. She had a U. of C. band on her wrist when found. She's in Emergency."

"Jesus." He covered his mouth with his hand and glanced at George. "On my way. 10-4." He placed the radio back in its holster, but before he took another step his cell phone rang.

"D? It's J.P. You have a minute?"

Chapter Forty-Four

Sam tidied the kitchen, putting the dishes, pans, and silverware back in their places after washing and drying. He took off his apron, folded it, and placed it in a drawer. "You ready?"

Fool, who hadn't lifted a finger, nodded. "You clean up the place real good, Sam. The old lady and I could use you. Ours has shit all over."

Sam eyed Fool with a questioning look, leaving the obvious unspoken. "There's clothes in the closet and bureau in the room where you slept. Take a few days' worth."

"Say what?"

Sam straightened. "Look, you can't wear the same things day in and day out. When and if we get to Chicago or anywhere else, you'll need clothes to wear."

"What makes you think I'm stick'n with you after finding the old lady?"

Sam stroked his chin. "Think about it."

"I am. I know the city better than you."

"Uh-huh. The parts you know, the cops know. I'd say your chances of (a) staying alive are slim, or (b) getting picked up, pretty good. You forget there's a warrant for your arrest, and your so-called 'friends' most likely shot your mother? They've made it clear they don't want you around."

Fool wasn't pleased to hear the crap about his future, particularly from Sam. No arguin', there was truth in what he say'n, but so what. Fool didn't play by other people's rules. If he had, he'd be dead a long time ago. He knew himself. He had that sixth sense that smelled shit before he stepped in it.

If Big was look'n to pop him, he'd somehow change it up. Big was a damn fool. All huff and not much puff. Stand up to the bastard and his dick gets soft like his head. As for the police…he'd stay low. They ain't knock'n themselves out to find him. In Chicago there's too many bad guys they're look'n for.

Fool put on a shit-eating grin. "You right, Sam, things don't look good for me." He shrugged. "They never do."

Sam picked keys from a tray. "That's fatalistic," he said over his shoulder. "I've told you before, planning makes the odds better. But you're a grown man. Do what you want."

Damn right. Fool followed him into the living room. He stopped and looked up at the bitchin' vaulted ceiling and stared at the skylights. *Holy shit.* "Come on, Sam, is this crib yours? I'll keep my trap shut about everything else."

Sam laughed. "No, you won't. You'll keep asking. I'm going upstairs to pack a few things. Coming?"

Fool's feet followed but his thoughts were stuck on the vaulted ceiling. He should have a look around the place before leaving. *Jesus this was so, so boss.* He took his time climbing the stairs, taking in the thick carpet and gliding his hand over the polished, smooth wood handrail. Reaching the top, he went down the hallway into the room with the bed that could probably sleep twelve. A chocolate leather duffel bag rested by the pillows. "What the hell?" He knew he didn't put it there. Nor did he own something that rich. "Sam?" He shouted. No response. *Damn, the walls were so thick, Sam didn't hear.* Fool stepped out, but Sam was nowhere in sight. *The man's a maniac, a fuck'n maniac who doesn't answer shit.* Fool went back in, shaking his head. He stood at the foot of the king-size mattress and sighed. *What the hell? So far, it's been a free ride. Whatever he gives me, I'll take.* He went to the closet and then the bureau and packed. The duffel bag was filled in no time and stretched to its limit. As he struggled with the zipper, he got the feeling someone was watching. "Damn this thing," and he slapped the side of it. "Sam—that you?" He straightened and turned toward the doorway.

"It's Samantha, if you must know, but you can call me Sammy."

"What the…?" He caught his breath staring at this woman about his age and height whose brownish hair went beyond her shoulders. She looked like the bitch in the *Little Mermaid* but with feet. "Who the fu… I mean where…did you…where's Sam?"

"You looked shocked." She had a serious look on her face, but her eyes sparkled.

"I am. Have you been here the whole time?"

"Depends on what you mean…whole time."

Fool stuffed a hand in his pocket. "You know…. this morning…last night…where the hell…Jesus." He rubbed his eyes. The more confused he became, the brighter her smile.

"May I?" She took a step into the room.

She had some kind of accent, but Fool couldn't place it. "Do what you want. Are you English?" She moved past and sat at the far corner of the bed. His eyeballs nearly popped. She had an ass perfectly outlined by the faded tight jeans; showing off legs that wouldn't quit. A fox if he ever saw one.

"No to your second question and as to your first, I arrived a few minutes ago. Sam asked me to assist him. You need to be driven to the pay phone and maybe Chicago."

Fool had his mouth open. He struggled to find words. "You…you know all that? Sam… told you?"

"I don't have telepathy."

Fool squinted, trying not to look or sound stupid. "Tele… tel… Did Sam tell you or he didn't?"

She went over to his duffle. "You can't just stuff things. You have to be strategic. She took several items out, folded them, placed them back inside, and zipped the bag closed. "Of course he told me."

Her smile dazzled.

"And just like that, you came. He snapped his fingers and here you are. This is blow'n my mind. Where's Sam, now?"

"I believe he left. Didn't he tell you?"

Fool blinked. *I got to sit. This is gett'n crazier and crazier.*

Chapter Forty-Five

Jasmine had no memory of how she got to this dark place sitting on a metal chair cuffed to a wall. She ached all over. The bandages over her other shoulder were half off and the smell clued her they needed to be changed. A single yellow bulb provided dim light. There were no windows as far as she could tell. Tape was over her mouth, but it wouldn't have made a difference. She had no energy to scream. She needed water. She needed to be back in the hospital. She needed…

Voices, then laughter from the far end of wherever she was. She strained to listen twisting her chained hand and sitting as erect as she could. Two men emerged from the darkness. They were talking fast to each other. She stared at them. One of them glanced at her, then ripped the gag from her mouth. She let out a small yelp.

"Can't give BJ's with her mouth covered," one said to the other. They laughed. Then the man who held the tape torn from her mouth stood over her. "Shut up, bitch. If you make noise again, we'll make sure it be the last you ever did."

She focused on the ivory handle tucked into the front of his pants. Big? He didn't look or sound like him. "I …wat…er. I…" She looked up at him. Her lips and body trembled.

"Look at that, the bitch is shakin'. We ain't goin' to hurt you." His smile curled his mouth. With his finger he lightly brushed her face. "No, ma'am. Maurice, get the lady water."

"Sure will, Tré. I'll let Leon know we back."

Trè grunted and waited until Maurice left. "Big told us you capped Shorty. Said you didn't want to put out for him. That true?"

Who the hell is this asshole? Her tongue, glued to the roof of her mouth, garbled her words. "W…a…t… t." She pulled on her handcuff.

"What you say'n?"

She couldn't point and she couldn't talk.

"What you gett'n all upset about? I asked a simple question."

Maurice returned with Leon.

"She ask'n for water. I think."

"Then give it to her. Don't want the bitch choke'n.... least not yet." Trè chuckled.

Maurice held her head and poured the cup. The water went down her throat too fast. She went into a coughing fit... sucking in air at the same time.

"She choke'n," Maurice dropped the cup, then slapped her back until the spasm stopped.

Her chest heaved. "I...I...ne...ed kle...enex. My... my...face."

Trè used two fingers to soak up Jasmine's mixture of tears and spittle, wiping the shit on the side of the sheet that covered her.

Leon glanced at Jasmine. "You sure you got the right bitch out of the hospital?" He grabbed her chin. "This Jasmine? She sure don't look it." He then snatched the dirty sheet and pulled it down. "Hmm... can't tell. Her titties look good, but..."

"Shut up." Trè gave Leon a little shove.

"Whatcha do that for? Just look'n."

"It's fuck'n Jasmine. Read the band on her wrist. M-a-n... Big was right about you, Leon. You think we'd take any bitch? We decided after we done Big..." Trè stopped, then began again. "We agreed Shorty ain't with us because one way or another she..."

"Ain't... true," Jasmine said in a croaky voice taking a breath after every word. "It ... Big...he .... shot...him... head. Big."

"Look at dem titties move," Leon licked his lips, then caught Trè's glare. "Big sure messed up." He moved several steps away and shrugged. "Got excited about what we go'n to do."

"Hold on. We can't fuck her the way she is." Maurice laid a hand on her unbandaged shoulder. "If we go'n to keep her, we need to get her fixed up. Shit, she got some kind of wound on her other side. It all bandaged. I don't want to fuck someone already fucked up."

"You got a point, Maurice." Trè rubbed his chin. "Give me a minute to think on it." He touched her face, then went down her front and grabbed a tit. It was firm and round. He let go and stepped back.

Jasmine 's arm pulled on the handcuff, but it only made a rattling noise. She wanted to spit but didn't have enough saliva.

"The bitch has some fight in her. That's good. Leon, unhook the cuff and stand her up. Maurice, get rid of the sheet. Let's see if she worth it."

"Wh...at ...you...doin'? What...you...want?" The Leon dude held her arm and the other two ripped her hospital bottoms off. She couldn't quite stand as the pain from her ribs and bullet wound had her bent. "Stop…p…l…e…a…s…e." She was beyond crying. She only had the strength to whimper even as one or maybe both grabbed her ass. Trè jabbed his finger in her pussy area.

"You…you…hurt'n…" She moved her leg to kick him, but he easily stepped away.

"You want to fight?" Trè rested his hand on the ivory handle tucked in his pants.

"I…," she breathed hard, "ain't…no…dog."

Trè straightened. "Let go of her arm, Leon, and take her in from the front. You too Maurice. What you think?" He glared at Jasmine. "Dogs get put down when they no use. You know that, right?" All three laughed.

* * *

"J.P., I'm in the middle of something, have to call you back." Dietrich held out his hand for George to wait.

"What's that?"

"I'm at U. of C. hospital checking on a shooting victim."

"Never a dull moment. I'm heading that way in a bit. My client's mom is also there. She was shot, too. Must be a pandemic."

"Very funny, but there's no cure. Is that the mom whose kid is in the wind? What's the name, again?"

"Yeah, one and the same…David Lanier, aka Fool."

"It's coming back to me. The white dude who acts gangsta."

"Right on target. No pun intended."

"It ain't a joke. I'll catch up with you later, J.P. Got to go." Dietrich pressed End on his phone and slipped it into his pants pocket. "Lead the way, George. Forget the Security Office for the moment. Need to get to Emergency."

George nodded. "Take elevator H, gets you right there." He pointed down the corridor.

Dietrich saw the sign with the letter H. "Thanks for your help. After I'm done with Emergency, will someone upstairs know where Security is?"

"Should, but your guess is as good as mine."

Dietrich had no trouble finding his way to the correct elevator. To his surprise, a car was waiting. Once inside, the panel had EMERGENCY First Floor in large letters. He punched the button, and unlike his earlier elevator experience, it was a smooth, quick ride. Several steps to his left was the waiting area. There was a large counter near the doors leading into the treatment facility. Dietrich quickened his pace, intending to ignore the desk personnel and walk through.

"You can't go in there," the large woman with orangey hair said in a tone indicating she had said that a hundred times. Her nametag read S. Jackson.

Dietrich flashed his badge. "Chicago Police."

The woman's expression soured further. "There's a whole slew of you guys in there. You late to the party?"

"Not really. I was here already looking for…never mind. Can I go in?"

She gave him a long look. "What's one more. Bay Twenty, but I doubt who you're look'n for is there. She better be in surgery. She was in poor shape when the ambulance brought her in."

Dietrich stopped at the door. "You have a name?"

Her face changed to surprise. "You know I can't tell you that. Sworn to what that call Hibert or somethin'. Uh-uh, can't say."

Dietrich took a deep breath. "Okay, you do'n your job like I'm doing mine. Got it." He hung his head for a moment.

"Don't feel so bad." She looked at her watch. "You know, I got to step away for a moment. I'll be back in a minute or two."

Dietrich watched her disappear down the hall. He waited a few seconds, then went behind her desk and scanned the entry sheet. "Ambulance, Maryweather, Sequia, f/b age 22 bullet wounds-C-22."

God damn, it isn't Jasmine. Where the hell is she?

Chapter Forty-Six

J. P. heard the click that ended his conversation with Dietrich and turned on his car's radio. Music, news, anything to take his mind off the situation. His doctor visit hadn't given him the air-tight defense he wanted, if Simone really went after him. At least he had documented the scratches on his back—ammunition to muddy the waters and create doubt.

The next step was to investigate court records to learn if Simone had done this kind of thing before. He had a hunch he had become her latest victim. He took a breath. His hand wavered over the call button that would phone his secretary. Easiest thing to do was to ask Tasha to look into it. He'd build his case against Simone and, once in a courtroom, he'd beat the shit out of her. The scenario felt good. Vindication… sweet.

His eye caught his speedometer. Geez, he was doing seventy in a forty-five. Better slow down, pal, he didn't need more problems. He let up on the gas and after checking his mirrors …. no cops. He let out a breath.

Courtroom. How long would it take to get his case to trial? He drummed his hand on the steering wheel. A year if lucky, and in that time, what happens to his practice…to him? All the years spent building his reputation shot to hell on a one-night dalliance. The press would be merciless. No privacy. His sex life, good and bad, would be broadcast to one and all. Nora and God knows who else could claim he did this or that. Simone might as well literally be crushing his balls. Was it worth the fight?

His thoughts went to his father who had worked for one of the steel mills on the outskirts of Chicago. The man always worked. Pops, after cashing his check from two weeks in the mills, would tell him, while holding a thick wad of cash, "Don't matter how much of these you got. What matters is how you got it and what you do with it. For some folks, it ain't never enough. For others…" He shrugged and then peeled off each bill, wetting his fingers to count his money. A broad grin crossed his face. "I ain't the richest, but doggone it, I ain't the poorest. It's honest and I sleep at night. It will do"

That was Pops. He had integrity and pride. Traits lost in today's noise. As Pops often said, "Money ain't everything."

Traffic slowed as J.P. took a curve in the road. The driver of the car next him was a youngish woman who smiled when their eyes met for an instant. She gave a half-hearted wave, then sped off. He didn't follow. Another Simone? He groaned and tightened his grip on the wheel.

What Simone claimed never happened. He wasn't that kind of a guy. He wasn't perfect, but he didn't sexually assault women. Never did, never would. He could almost hear Pop's "amen" echo in his ear. *Okay then.* He pressed on the gas. The car accelerated. The well-tuned machine felt like riding a thoroughbred. With an eye on the road, he ticked off things he needed to do. He'd have to patch things up with Nora. He didn't know how, but he'd have to try again. He checked the clock on the instrument panel; 4:20 p.m., then took a deep breath. "Call Tasha," he ordered the car's computer.

* * *

Simone returned to her office. Her walk from her doctor's office and the stop at Starbucks released some of the tension she always felt at the beginning of these affairs. She sat at her desk, her office door closed and waited. Now and then, she eyed the clock resting on the corner. A pad of paper was in front of her as well as the original of the Agreement she had given J.P.

For some damn reason, Sol was still on her mind. The sonofabitch was dead...dead for a long time. How could their tryst still plague her? Ach, she had moved on. Sol had done her a favor. He pierced her idea...the purity of love. No such thing and her history proved it. It was time to get real. There was a lot on the line.

She stared at her Yurman silver bracelet, then fondled it. This period between her accusation and a man's capitulation electrified her with excitement—the peering into the unknown.

What was J.P. thinking? She understood his process well. First there was shock, then indignation. "How could she, that bitch. I'll take her for everything she's worth. I'm not that kind of guy." She sighed. How well worn… how pathetic. She pictured J.P. seething with anger and even a little embarrassment.

A "player" like J.P. doesn't see himself on the defensive. He's the one making the moves, believing he can smooth-talk his way into any woman's panties and get away with it. "She wanted it, Judge. She led me on." Simone yawned.

At some point, the poor dear feels squeezed. The realization of her accusations grabs him. His eyes display fear and pain. What if this becomes public? He pictures his ruination. His hands sweat and there's a lump in his throat. There goes his business, his reputation, his friends, not to say the least, his wife or lover. All those things weigh on him and the will to fight recedes. What's a few bucks to keep this mess quiet. No one else has to know. One lousy check and all this goes away. She smiled. After all, what was money for if not to buy things, especially peace of mind.

Chapter Forty-Seven

"We goin' now?" Fool was resigned to hear more bullshit. Between the casino, Sam, and now her … whatever her name, he was up a river without a paddle. He couldn't decide a damn thing for himself any longer. He had no wheels, not much cash, or knew where the hell he was.

He wiped his face with his hands. He could feel the bitch staring at him. Was he dream'n?

"Are you coming along or just going to sit on the edge of the bed, moping?"

Fool peeked between his fingers at this…this woman who tossed her hair to the side, then reached for his duffel. She was close enough to touch. Jesus Christ, the perfume the bitch wore made him hard. And he thought Jasmine was a seven or eight. He really didn't know shit about the world.

"Guess so. You the boss." He took a moment to get up from the bed.

"Not really, David, I'm doing Sam a favor. That's all. Now let's get crack'n."

She carried his bag and led the way. He followed as if he was under a spell. They went down the stairs, through the living room, then the kitchen. When not staring at her ass, he checked for signs of Sam. There weren't any.

They entered the garage through a door off the eating area.

"Holy shit."

"What was that?"

"You're driving an M840i Beamer convertible. That's a lot of coin."

She shrugged. "One of the perks, I guess. Get in."

He did as told. His gaze fixed on her.

"What's the matter with you, David? You act as if you've never seen a woman before. It's kind of creepy, you know."

He could feel his face get hot. "Don't mean noth'n by it. Too many things happen'n: Sam, the crap in Chicago, my old lady, now you. I mean you seem nice and…more than…shit, just take me to the damn phone."

"Did I offend you in some way?" She pressed a button, and the garage door opened. "Up or down?"

"Huh?"

"The top. It's a convertible."

"I ain't stupid. Said that when I saw the ride. It's not summer."

"So, don't you want the wind in your hair? The automobile has a heater. Besides…," she smiled, "you won't have to worry about talking to me."

She hit the gas. The car roared in reverse, then came to a screeching stop at the end of the driveway.

"Well?"

Goddamn her. "Do what you want."

"You're not at all what Sam described." She hit another lever and the top came down. "I'll turn up the heat. Let me know when you're hot."

She drove like Sam once they got on the highway. Speed limit signs were only a suggestion. "Don't tell me you work for BMW," he said glancing at the speedometer.

"What? BMW?"

"I said…" Her hair flew in the wind, and she brushed some from her mouth. "What do you do for BMW?"

"Nothing. Why?"

Fool shrugged, then yelled, "Forget it. Aren't you worried about cops?" He pointed.

She turned toward him. "Not really. There aren't any this way."

Even though it was night when Sam drove him to that coin-eating phone booth, he sensed the highway was different. He was sure Sam drove on a four-lane. He had seen interstate signs; theirs were two and the signs…state highways.

"You are taking me to make my call?" He looked over at her concentrating on the road.

"Yeah, sure. Why are you asking?"

"'Cause we're going a different way."

"Not a problem, David. There is more than one way to a destination. The less populated the road, the less possible trouble. You agree?"

She did it again. She left him nothing to say, but "Yes". He nodded, and she went back to driving.

The wind stung his eyes, and he didn't like his hair all messed up. He stared at the passing scenery for a minute, rubbed his eyes, then fought to keep his do in place. *Should have worn a hat.* He stole a look at her, working up his courage.

"What's your story? You know, Sam…and…" He moved his hand in a circle. "This."

She didn't respond. He figured she didn't hear. He leaned over the center console. "I said what's up with you and Sam?"

She momentarily glanced at him. "I've been thinking, we're wasting time taking you to the pay phone."

"Huh? What about the pay phone?"

"Too many what if's—getting through, your lawyer, condition of your mother."

The damn wind made hearing difficult. He stretched farther. She didn't seem to notice as she looked at the road.

"I say forget all that, David. Nothing is accomplished by that call. There's no upside." She turned and faced him. "We'll go straight to the problem…Chicago." She took a second, it seemed, to digest her decision, then gunned the car, laying a streak of rubber.

Chapter Forty-Eight

Leon stroked the thin hairs of a wanna-be beard on his chin, then nodded. "I think with a little white powder; the bitch can still put out." He walked around her and put a hand on the small of her back. "She could take us pretty good."

"Yeah, maybe but it ain't goin' to happen today." Maurice swiped his hand on Jasmine's tit. "She got those going for her."

Jasmine didn't react to Maurice or the other comments. She kept her eyes on Trè. His hand rested on that ivory handle gun in his waistband. It didn't take much to realize Trè ran the show. Didn't know what happened to Big, but if he no longer breathin', he deserved what he got.

She straightened herself despite the hurt. Her chest stood out. She had curves in the right places and was getting a rise out of them. "Let me be for today." Her voice shook. She took a minute. "I'll do y'all tomorrow." Each breath painful but she worked hard not to show it. "I'll fuck the daylights out of..."

"Shut up," Trè held her jaw between his forefinger and thumb. "You talk too much. It ain't your business what we do or don't." He applied pressure, then let go.

She fought not to rub the spot. Trè didn't give a shit if she lived or died. She was an item to him and the other scum. A thing to be used as a prize.

It was clear to her if she couldn't be a whore, they'd kill her. They might do that anyway, but she'd buy time.

"Cuff her to the wall."

"What about her clothes? She could get cold." Maurice stooped to pick up the sheet and undergarments.

Trè glanced at his crew. "Who the fuck cares."

"Hold on, Trè. If she gets sick, she ain't no good to us.

Trè rested his hand on the ivory handle. "All right. Keep her naked for a while. Use the sheet if she starts to shiver. Leon, you watch her. Don't do anything stupid until Maurice and I decide."

"I'll tell you my vote right now."

"I know your vote. It's your dick that's think'n. Do what I tell you and don't fuck up."

Leon yanked Jasmine's good arm behind her and pushed her on the chair where she'd been handcuffed. He busied himself making sure she couldn't wriggle her wrist out of it. After a tug or two, he stepped to her side. He strained his neck making sure Trè and Maurice had moved away. "Just you and me, bitch."

The look on his face made her sick. What was wrong with the life she had with Fool. Not enough excitement? See if her shit was better than anyone. Who was the fool now? If she had any chance of surviving this nightmare, this was it. The little man was packin' and it was in his back pocket. Somehow… "Leon, that what you called?"

He looked around and stood a little closer. "Yeah."

"Leon, I did you real good, didn't I?"

A smile broke over his face. "You sure did…sure as hell did." He pounded his fist into his hand.

"Well…" She moved closer as best she could. "I … you know…" Her eyes were on his pants zipper.

"Say what? I thought you pussy ain't work'n…besides there's no time."

"More than one way to get you off, but I'll need my arm. I'll make you feel so, so g-o-o-d." She caught her breath. *G-d, the pain,* and gritted her teeth. She got to keep play'n, focusing on what can save her.

"Nah…nah, I…" Leon grabbed her tit. "Jesus, it sweet." He moved several steps away and disappeared into the darkness. Seconds later he reappeared, unlocked the handcuff, then unbuckled his jeans. His pants slid down. "All right bitch, do it."

* * *

Dietrich stood over Ms. Jackson's desk and took a second look at the information on the emergency room entry sheet, while keeping an eye out for Jackson's return. The age of the patient was about right as well as the sex but the name, Sequia Maryweather …not even close. He glanced at the address where the ambulance found this person. It was listed as 45th and Justine. He compared it to what he had previously written in his notes for Jasmine's home. They were miles apart, although that didn't necessarily rule her out, but it certainly was another fact in the negative column. He spotted Ms. Jackson walking back at a slow pace and moved away from the desk.

She took her time but eventually got to her workstation. "Everything all right?" She looked at Dietrich but didn't wait for an answer. "I needed that break. The things that go on in here." She shook her head. "Jesus, have mercy." She pulled her chair out from under the desk and plopped down with a gasp.

"Yes, ma'am. Everything is cool. Can I go in?"

She pressed a button that opened the door. "You have a good day."

Dietrich hurried through and mumbled, "Thanks". It wasn't difficult to find Sequia's assigned patient bay as two other cops and a female policewoman waited around an empty bed.

"Dietrich, Fourth District," he said by way of introducing himself. "I was following up another shooting with a possible shooter or…" he glanced at the gurney, "or victim. Any info on this Sequia?"

The female officer, Daniels, spoke up. "A neighbor claimed, he heard an argument over some damn chicken or turkey bone. Stepdad got pissed and is in the wind. Another day in paradise."

"Ain't that right." Dietrich stroked his chin and went for a Hail Mary. "Any of you know if Sequia went by any other name?"

"Need prints for that," Daniels pointed out. She looked at her partners.

"Don't have a clue," one of them answered. "We didn't do any of the investigating, only followed the ambulance."

Dietrich heard cries of other patients in the partitions near him but didn't react. It was all part of the milieu. Instead, he joined his fellow officers in war stories about their jobs. Their guffaws were in stark contrast to the surroundings. Any diversion to pass the time.

Dietrich poked his head out from the curtain that enclosed the space. Not seeing anyone approaching, he stepped back into the bay. "How much longer?"

Daniels looked away from studying her fingernails and checked her watch. "We've been here, what, an hour? I'd give it another thirty minutes."

One of the male cops, Collins, eyed his partner, Shu, then shook his head. "Shit, no. If it goes past an hour, we're in for longer than that." He leaned back in his chair then glanced at the ceiling… two hours. "Yep,

I'd say we got two more hours."

Shu agreed.

Daniels smiled. "What do you say, Dietrich?"

"Me?" He shrugged.

"Come on, you have to have an opinion."

"Okay, forty-five."

"Hours?"

"Minutes."

Daniels moved toward the gurney. "Let's put some chump change on it?"

"You got to be kidding." Dietrich scratched his head.

"We'll have two bets. One, how long, and the other, if she's dead or alive when the doc gets here."

"Holy shit. You are cold."

It was her turn to shrug. "Everyone put in a ten. We'll keep it civil."

Chapter Forty-Nine

In the late afternoon, Dr. Hanson tapped on Anne's hospital door, 3737, then went in. The TV was on, and she was sitting in her bed.

"Feeling a bit better?"

A small smile crossed her face. "I guess. It feels like someone sawed off my left side."

Hanson pulled the guest chair closer to her. "Yeah, it will take a while. I can up the morphine if you'd like."

She shook her head. "It's bearable… a painful reminder of what happened."

"Speaking of that, I did some digging. The good news, according to our computer: there's a Jasmine Taylor at this hospital. That's her last name, right?

Anne wondered if she ever knew that. She thought hard. "I think so. David, my son, may have mentioned it."

"She's on the floor below you."

Anne pressed a hand to her mouth. "She is? Why? What happened?"

Hanson hesitated, "HIPAA," then shrugged. "I don't think I'm violating it as it's in the news. She was shot."

"No!"

"I can only tell you, she's alive. I don't know anything else."

"Oh my God. Terrible." It hurt like hell when she took a deep breath. "Can I see her?"

"Information has her on the second floor, 2604, but you're in no condition to move."

"Can I call?"

"Sure, but I'd give it a day."

"That serious."

Hanson looked away. "Unfortunately, I can't say."

"Thank you for at least that. What about…" her eyes began to tear, "Charise."

"I'm afraid she didn't make it. I'm sorry."

Tears flowed. "I'm…I…had…a…"

Hanson grabbed several tissues from the box on a table near him. "Take it easy, Anne," and wiped her face.

She gulped air and fought to steady herself. "Damn this hurts."

"I'll get you more pain killers."

"She was a good, good person," Anne said through gritted teeth.

Hanson got up. "I'm sure she was." He touched her shoulder. "It's your job to take care of yourself. I'll check on you later."

She wiped her eyes and blinked a few times. "Thank you, Doctor."

He took a step toward the door.

"Can I trouble you for my phone? I think it's on the side table."

"Sure." He walked over and, after moving a plastic water pitcher that spilled a little water, gave it to her. "Don't be on this thing for long. You need your rest."

She tried to salute. "Aye, aye."

He left and the silence of the room was stifling. She eyed her cell. There were no messages for her. Why would there be? Charise was dead, David was…oh poor David. She'd try him again. Maybe he came home and didn't know. She punched in his number and listened to the beeps.

How fast her world had crumbled…one day…that was all it had been. A mere twenty-four hours that felt like years. Her son, her friend, Jasmine, the pain of loss deeper than any wound.

There was no answer. Wherever David was, his phone wasn't with him. She hung up and let her cell slip from her hand to her chest. She was alone, similar to the day Sol died. But then… Her lips trembled, and her hand tightened around the bedsheet. She didn't want to dig into those memories. They were useless but her brain didn't listen. She closed her eyes. There was Sol dangling in the garage, and David gaping. She steeled herself to make the phone calls to the family. As days went by, she found Sol's handwritten notes and recalled a phone call warning that Simone, her friend, had betrayed her. Shit, she was dealt some bad cards.

In the past, she had wondered why she didn't feel anger toward Sol or even Simone. Why, it was more like an acceptance. She knew her arguments well.

That was the situation—he cheated on her, there was nothing more she could do about it now, when the fucker was dead. They deceived her. It wasn't unique. Had she suspected? She wasn't blind or stupid. She heard the whispers, was aware of the signs and all, but ignored them. It was easier not to see what could be seen. Besides, the romance of youth wasn't her focus after years of marriage. Happiness, sexual gratification gave way to making a living, raising a child. Was that wrong?

Charise would chide her: "All that is sensible, but girl, you have to have fun in your life. Your man needs to be taken care of, otherwise..." and her gaze would wander off.

Anne opened her eyes. Now there was no Charise, no David, and God knows about Jasmine. She stared into space. Charise would tell her to do something—anything. "If you want to find David...Jasmine may know where. She's only a floor below. Get your ass off that bed, girl." That would be Charise: take charge and no moping. God, you're going to get an earful from her.

Anne regulated her breathing, to keep the pain minimal. How was she going to maneuver herself to reach Jasmine's room, if she couldn't even turn on her side. Answer that, Charise. Anne slapped the bed cover with her one good hand. Her phone bounced off her chest toward her stomach. *Charise, I'd give anything to hear your voice.* Maybe it was a hallucination, given all the drugs she was taking, but Anne heard Charise, or something like her. Whatever it was, it made Anne fumble for her cell. If she wasn't able to see Jasmine, there was someone else who could. The number was on her speed dial.

Chapter Fifty

"You're say'n you're the one taking me to Chicago?" Samantha's heavy foot on the gas pressed Fool into his seat by the G-force she created. "S-h-i-t."

"Don't make a face, David. I'm very capable." She patted the console cover. "I know how to use one and can hit a target within fifty feet."

He stared. "The hell...you're packing?" Did he have her all wrong? Was the bitch some character out of *Mr. and Mrs. Smith?* She being Mrs. Smith.

"I suppose you also know kung fu or some other crap."

"I do okay in the martial arts. Always room for improvement."

There goes that smile of hers. "What about Sam?"

"What about him? He trusts my judgement."

"He does, does he? Do I have a say?"

She gave him a quick glance. "I thought you were worried about your mother?"

"I am...but." He swept his face with his hand. "I..."

"You thought it would be you and Sam on this trip?"

"Yeah. I did."

"Things change...get accustomed to it."

Fool stared out his window. His right hand balled into a fist. The car whizzed by several telephone poles before he turned back to Samantha. "I want to talk to Sam. I don't know you from Adam."

"You don't know Sam, either."

She had him there.

He swallowed hard. He was tired of being on the losing end of every conversation. "Look, I'm in enough shit without getting caught in more. Stop the fuck'n ride and I'll make my way. I don't need you, Sam, or anybody. I shouldn't have gone along with that crazy dude in the first place. Tell him thanks and all, but I'm done. Pull over."

Samantha didn't take her eyes off her driving. "David, we're on back roads in the middle of nowhere. Are you think'n of walking to Chicago?

We're one hundred and forty miles away. It's a nice hike for anyone. If you did twenty miles a day, you'd be there in what…a week? By that time, who knows the condition of your mother. You want to chance that?"

"I ain't play'n. Stop the car." He had leaned on the console working to open it.

"It's locked." She slowed the vehicle and kicked up dirt and stones coming to a stop off the side. "Before you open that door, you impulsive snit, think about the larger issue."

He could feel his face get hot. Another fuck'n lecture? Screw her. His mind raced. What if he punched her out, then took the Beamer.

"Did you think of who shot your mother?"

That stopped him. "Say again?"

"Who was the asshole who shot your mother. Do you know? Did you think about it?"

"Yeah, and yeah. It had to be Big and his crew. Same ones who fucked Jasmine."

"Your girlfriend?"

Even though he had complained about being cold and riding in a convertible, he was sweating. He used his sleeve to wipe his forehead. *What was Samantha getting at?* He unclenched his hands. "You could say. She was sort of my girl."

Another smile. She brushed a strand of hair from her mouth. "So, she was your girlfriend who, I think the phrase is, these monsters pulled a train on her. Don't you want to do something?"

He felt his junk quiver, wanting to crawl into his body and hide. He hadn't thought much about Jasmine since that scene at the Q and Jerk. That was a lie, but hell, she didn't make much of an effort to get out of the place. Maybe he had it all wrong. She didn't leave because those fuckers wouldn't let her. Big's message to him was not only get out of town but he was taking everything Fool had, his girl, his mother, and next would be his life. He couldn't come back to Chicago unless he dealt with Big and his shitheads.

Fool rubbed his face, then looked straight at Samantha. "What are you say'n? We're not going to see my old lady?"

"Come on, David, you're not dumb. Yes, we're going to see your mother, but…"

Fool's stomach did a turn. The bitch really was fuck'n crazy. Big would crush them like a damn bug on the wall.

"You're never going to be safe unless you confront those bastards. Surprise is our greatest weapon. I'm sure your arrival is one they would never expect."

"True enough, but Big ain't alone."

"Even better. Disbelief and speed overcome a lot. Big and his cohorts disrespected you. They view you as a threat to them and they won't stop until they put you in the ground."

"Jesus Christ, how you come up with that?"

"Just analyzing the situation. Your court case set this in motion."

"Huh? What?"

"I read. Your little disappearance act from Chicago and history was not only on the news but in the papers. I put two and two together. A trial would reveal you were set up. Big wants you either to take the fall or..."

Fool's jaw dropped. In all the months with his mouthpiece, J.P., he never put it as squarely as this...this woman did in a minute. Where the hell did Sam find her?

"Lady, you have balls."

"I believe you're giving me a compliment, and it's Samantha."

"All right... Samantha," he shrugged. "Yeah, it was a compliment." He congratulated himself that she got it. "You better be what you say, otherwise..."

"I'm damn good. I know I don't look the part, but...," she laughed, "that's how I get them. You with me?"

Fool glanced at the farmland spread out before him. He drummed his hand on his lap. "To be or not to be?"

"Oh my God, you're quoting Hamlet. Shakespeare?"

Fool knew his face heated up again. "Nah. Must have heard it in a tune or something. Shakespeare? Nothing like that. He a relative of yours?"

Samantha gave him a long look. Fool knew how to play poker and returned her stare.

"Doesn't matter. Where do these bastards hang out?"

This time Fool smiled. "You're beginning to talk my way. Big stays around Seventy-eighth and Coles. He does his hustle out of there."

"Let's pay him a visit. The sooner he's out of the way, the more room we have to operate."

"Operate, like take'n his territory?"
"No, no. The safer you are."

Chapter Fifty-One

Jasmine opened one eye, then the other. She had no memory of how long she had been lying on the cement floor or how she got there. The cold and harshness of it must have seeped through her naked body and awakened her. She raised herself a few inches and saw a Glock where her outstretched arm had been. Gasping for breath, she was able to see a man's face not far from the weapon. He didn't seem to be moving. "L-e-o-n?" It hurt like hell to spit out his name. "L-e-e..." Her strength ebbed and she sank back down, panting. *What the fuck happened?* She began to shiver. She needed to get up or at least sit. *How am I goin' to do that when I can't lift my head?* Her teeth chattered. *Gotta get.* "Leon, get me up...Tre`... Maurice." Her plea went nowhere. She gulped in air, and with the strength she had left rolled herself onto her back. Blood drenched her good hand as she touched the wound in her lower stomach. *The motherfuckers shot me.* She was sweating and freezing at the same time. *This ain't good. Jesus.* She whimpered, holding back tears. No sense wasting energy. She wanted to remember. *If the Lord is going to take me then at least give me the strength to recall.* She closed her eyes. Her lips quivered. Through force of will, bits and pieces of what took place came back.

Leon unbuckled his belt and jeans.

"Leon, you gonna stick that thing in my mouth?"

He held his dick in one hand and with his pants down around his knees, moved toward her. "Fuck'n A, bitch. Now do your thing."

She watched him get close enough, then kicked him in his balls. He sank down screaming. She amazed herself at her speed going for his gun jutting out of his back pocket. The place exploded with voices, shouts... She stood, damn fool she was, and fired. Didn't know how many times. Something hot pierced her and she fell. There were groans all around her. The last voice she heard after hitting the floor was Trè. "Pussy ain't worth shit, Leon," then silence.

She blinked a few times looking up at an endless blackness. She had done good. Those fuckers didn't know who they were dealing with. Lying on her back, an enfolding cuddling warmth replaced the chills she had moments before. She was no longer bothered by the floor's dampness and cold. A wave of contentment came over her as she placed her hand on her chest.

Fool wouldn't believe what she had done. She told him she knew how to shoot after one of them lazy days together. Fool had raised his eyes, "Uh-huh." He'd be a believer, now. She had a good thing with him. She hoped Fool and Momma Lanier would forgive her and prayed Shorty and Big didn't do Ms. Anne much harm.

A burning sensation surged from her stomach to her shoulder. *Oh, man am I on fire?* She used her good hand to feel around. There was no fire…no nothing. Her mind playing tricks, that's all. She reached out to touch Fool. Her hand, suspended in the air, searched for his face. He seemed so real but he too… gone. Her thoughts shifted. Fool's image faded replaced by Tré in full strut. Inspecting her like a prize cow with his two assholes ready to jump her. She heard herself tell them, "I'd fuck you good tomorrow if you let me be today." Should have known they'd always want today. Tomorrow was something they ain't seen and didn't know.

A tear trickled down her face. No sense wiping it away. What was done was done. Her breathing became shallow—ready for a long sleep. A half smile crept across her parched chapped lips. Her hand fell to the side. She was as good as her word, though. She fucked them good…real good.

* * *

"Somethin' ain't right." Fool stared in the direction of Big's garage. "Ain't no lights, ain't anyone hanging around. Not the way it be this time of day."

Samantha had driven around the block twice. "Are you sure we're at the right place?"

He gave her a cold stare. "I know my hood. I know the rhythm of it. Today ain't no holiday and no one is in church. I'm feel'n somethin' bad."

She made one more pass, then found a space a few doors down from the garage and parked. "We'll wait. It shouldn't be much longer before dark. If the situation stays the same, we'll go in."

"We'll what? You don't think this ride and you ain't drawin' attention? We're sittin' like ducks on a pond. Anyone who looks knows we're out of place."

"David, either they'll believe we're some undercover cops or two white kids from the suburbs looking to buy. In either case, we'll be all right."

If she was nervous or scared, she didn't show it. Thank God, he persuaded her to put the top up.

"On any other night," Fool told her, "there would be a stream of homies knock'n on the small door on the side of Big's garage."

"Were they able to enter the garage willy-nilly? That would be dumb, but..."

"Big and his assholes aren't stupid. You had to know the rap to be let in." Fool rubbed his chin. "I remember it was four times–two rapid, a pause, then two more repeated twice the same way."

"Whew, a secret code. That's thinking." She made a face that Fool ignored.

"Hey, you want to know how it's done. Listen up."

"All right, only kidding around. Yes, I want to know." She turned serious.

"One of Big's crew, usually Leon, would look through the slot in the door. He wasn't the brains, but he had a nose for who didn't look right. Maurice usually did the packaging, while Big and Shorty and sometimes Trè would drive in Big's Caddy scouting the hood.

"Times when there was no traffic around the joint, the word got out a meeting was happen'n. Sometimes it would get crazy, and a motherfucker would start scream'n about something he didn't like or felt dissed. Good thing their pieces were checked at the door. After whatever business was discussed, those meetings turned into a hell of a party—you name the drug, it was there, as well as booze and of course bitches and ho's. That would usually be Leon's job to round them up. Only time he got to drive the Caddy."

"What's the difference between them?"

Fool saw she wasn't joking. "Ho's put out for scratch, bitches want to be seen and be part of an entourage."

"Oh... okay. You think there's a meeting?"

Fool gave it some thought. "A possibility, but ain't seen the Caddy or any other cars pulling up, honking their horns, or bitches in tight… I mean, ladies in thigh-high skirts and …"

"I get the picture."

"You ever been in the city? You seem to be a nice suburban girl who would never be in this part of town."

"For your information, I grew up in lots of places—cities, suburbs, even spent time on a farm."

"Huh. Your daddy in the army or something?"

She eyed him, then glanced straight ahead. "Something like that. Didn't stay in any one place long. Got to see the country, though. I learned about people and that's an education in itself." She turned and unlocked the center console. "Time to go," and took out the Beretta, placing it in the holster at the small of her back. "It's dark enough. Ready to party?" Her eyes sparkled and a tight smile crossed her face.

"You are something else." Fool opened his door and waited for her on the sidewalk. "I'll lead."

Chapter Fifty-Two

J.P. glanced at the clock in his car. He figured there was about thirty minutes left before Simone's deadline. After having Tasha work on Simone's past, the next thing to check off the list was Nora. He should stop by her office at 26th Street before she left for the day. Pay Anne a visit? She wasn't going anywhere. His car phone interrupted his thoughts. He picked up without looking at the caller I.D.

"Yeah, Tash, what did you find?"

A male voice responded. "It's Dietrich, remember your friendly neighborhood copper."

J.P. collected himself. "Dietrich…sorry. Thought my secretary was calling. What's up?"

"You said you were on your way to the hospital. I need a favor."

"What's that?"

"I need you to identify someone who was shot."

"Did Anne die?"

"Who? You mean Lanier's mother? I don't know about that. Haven't had time to check her out. I'm asking about Jasmine Taylor. Your client or should I say former client's woman."

"I'm still his lawyer. Jasmine? What's she doing at the hospital?"

"Long story, I'll fill you in when you get here. I've told Emergency to expect you. What's your e.t.a.?"

"Shit," J.P. uttered under his breath, then glanced at the clock again. "I can be there in about thirty minutes."

"Great. See you then. Remember, Emergency, bay twenty."

J.P. eyed the road. "Got it. Bay twenty. See you."

He disconnected, then drummed his hand on the steering wheel. Where was that fool, David, if Jasmine was dead? Next question: would he have been involved? If he was… damn, there goes his case. He's a goner. The judge will send him away forever. He slowed down and searched for a place to stop. He found one near a fire hydrant. He shrugged. What the hell…he wasn't parking. Next thought—call Tasha.

He ordered his phone to do so. She picked up after two rings.

"Hey, it's me. Find anything on Simone?"

"You called me five minutes ago. No, I'm not that fast."

"Hmm." His eyes darted to the clock on his instrument panel. "You're right. Any calls from David Lanier? The State's Attorney Office?... Nora?"

"Nope. I would have phoned you if they did."

"Right. Can't blame a guy for hoping."

"Your client and you will need more than hope."

J.P. tightened his hold on the steering wheel. She got that straight. Hope without action doesn't go far. He stared out the driver's window. "Thanks, Tash."

"Where are you, anyway?"

The question caught him off-guard. He scanned his GPS for guidance. "I'm on Martin Luther King Dr. about twenty-two hundred south."

"Curious way of getting to Hyde Park and U. of C. Hospital."

"Well...I...if you find anything in the next few minutes let me know."

"Sure will."

J.P. wiped his face with his hand. His world until now ran effortless. He was the golden boy. The son who could do no wrong because he went further than anyone in his family. His hand smoothed out his overcoat. He wore custom-made from the finest wool and sometimes cashmere. He earned more money in a week than his poor old pop did working the mills for several months. Why? Because he knew the system and was a winner.

He stared at the fire hydrant for a moment. Jesus. Was he daring to be caught? A half smile crossed his face. Luck and skill—a great combination. One needed both to bear fruit.

His attention turned to the clock on his dash. It was ticking down like some mope who stood before the court waiting for his sentence with a judge who handed out years like candy.

J.P. sighed and looked at his watch. It was getting closer to five. He leaned back in his seat and shut his eyes. What was Simone thinking? Another trophy? Damn her.

He balled his hand into a fist, then unclenched and pushed the window button. The street air blew in. The sharpness of it caught his face and sent a chill. He wasn't going down like some poor schmuck caught in the headlights. Why not let Simone wait? There's nothing magic about her deadline. Fuck her five o'clock. His Pop often told him, "Son, get your priorities. The rest is noise." *The old man was right again.* He had more important things to do.... people pinned their hopes on him. Whatever hell awaited him, he'd make sure Simone would be there with him. As for now he had other responsibilities.

Deep inside him, he was aware he was crossing a line. Never take it home with you. Don't make the cases personal. Well, they have. Lives were at stake. For one of the first times in his life came the realization that money and what it bought weren't enough. Maybe he had Simone to thank. Maybe he would rue this day. But he wasn't going to play Simone's game. There was no reason to respond to her bullshit accusations. What he needed to do was get to the hospital. What he had to do was make amends with Nora—but for the right reason.

* * *

Tired of sitting at her desk, Simone needed to move. Nerves played a part but the lack of visiting the fitness center was the real culprit. She began to pace back and forth in her twelve-by-sixteen office to the point where she accumulated several hundred steps. She acquainted herself with every inch of the place. Saw dust balls hidden behind several pieces of furniture. After the ninth or was it the tenth time around, she'd had enough and decided to leave. She forwarded her office phone to her cell, then checked her watch. Forty minutes to go, plenty of time to make it home and prepare herself and the scene, in case...

She threw on her coat and locked the door. The trip to the main floor took a minute or two. Once outside, she hailed a cab. She was old-fashioned in that way. Uber services were too personal—credit card, phone records, and all. Taxis, on the other hand, still used cash and were anonymous.

Traffic was the usual congestion. She comforted herself during the ride with the knowledge that some men took more time than others to reach the right conclusion. Some liked to play it near the edge, thinking they'd give her a whiff of her own medicine. In the end, though... she grinned, she got the happy ending.

She arrived home with several minutes to spare. She went upstairs to the bedroom where last night's affair took place. She hadn't moved a thing. Her torn clothing was strewn on the plush rug where J.P. attacked her. The chaise longue, the scene to the prelude of the assault, was unmade, the pillows knocked around in still-life formations. Her gaze went from there to the glasses of liquor that lay on the hard wood floor. The fluids had spotted the area near the rug. She thought that was a nice touch.

She rehearsed her lines: J.P. had suggested a drink. She told him the bar was on the floor below. She lost track of how long he spent there, and eventually he returned with two glasses. She said she didn't really want one, but he persisted. God only knows, if he put something in them.

The detective would hide behind a blank face. "Go on, Ms. Jenwick, what happened then?"

She would pause, her voice becoming husky, her hand trembling. The words would be labored, as she delved into the terrible act J.P. committed against her.

The cops would want evidence, her torn clothes, the liquor glasses, and her doctor's report.

Satisfied with her story, if it came to that, she glanced at her watch. It was five to five. The fucker was testing her whether she really meant to go through with it. J.P. probably was hunkered over his phone cussing at it, praying it would ring, praying she'd say she'd thought about it, and concluded not to go after him. She chuckled—what a little man. He had better wise up soon. She took one more look at the scene, satisfied all was ready, and made her way from the bedroom to her first-floor office off the kitchen. She grabbed the chair from behind her desk and turned on her 50" TV with the remote.

Two minutes to go. She leaned back and closed her eyes. A hundred and seventy-five thousand dollars, not a king's ransom, but a fair price for a night's work. A girl could certainly pamper herself with that kind of extra cash. A vacation in Tuscany, a little shopping in Paris, a nicer car… a Lexus maybe, only the best, J.P.—only the best.

Chapter Fifty-Three

Fool twisted the knob on the side door of Big's garage. The door opened, just like that. "Somethin' ain't right. Didn't even use the code."

Samantha eyed him with a quizzical look. "What's the big deal?"

"No one ever walked in. One of Big's crew would have been peek'n through the door slot. They ain't never left it unlocked."

"You should know. Move in. We can't just stand here."

He glared. "I'm tell'n you. You need to understand this shit."

They entered.

"You smell that?"

Samantha stopped and sniffed. "Whatever that odor is, is…

"You're smellin' acrid sulfurous odor and blood. Someone been popped."

"What the hell are you talking about?"

"Jesus, Samantha—guns. There's been shooting in here. Hush your voice."

He nudged her. "Look over there parked by the staircase," his voice low. "That's Big's Caddy." He pointed through the murky light, holding his nose. "That's his love, the mother-fucker. Everyone in the hood knew Big was comin' when he drove that thing."

Samantha nodded. "I bet the police did too." She had a "gotcha" expression on her face.

"I guess that's right. No more conversation."

They stepped toward the ride. It was dark and he slipped on something wet and lost his balance. He fell and saw Big's head sticking out from underneath the car. He sat up, wiping his bloody hands on his pants. "Jesus fuck'n Christ. Big been popped."

"He's dead?" Samantha said, her voice steady.

"You got that right." He got up and put his finger toward his lips, signaling quiet. They went deeper into the garage. Samantha used her phone for a light. They almost stepped on Trè.

"Holy crap." Fool kneeled and saw a Glock near Très hand. "What the fuck?"

"Look over here," Samantha was a few feet in front. "There's two more and a girl."

He followed. "Jasmine—oh my God." She had one hand resting on her chest. Her eyes stared blankly at some unknown spot on the ceiling. His knees buckled. A shock of heat followed by a coldness went through him. He heaved. Vomit splattered on her body.

"So much for the crime scene." Samantha grabbed David by his shoulders.

"Who the hell cares," his words spilled out. "Fuck the bastards... killed... they... oh shit, shit, oh my God. She's dead, Samantha, Jasmine is dead."

Samantha helped him up and led him out of the garage while he babbled, cried, and was useless. Where they spent that night and the ones after was all a blur. He didn't go and see his mother, then at the hospital. Instead, for days on end, he'd wake scared shitless visualizing Jasmine's lifelessness. Days afterwards it hit him; he could be lying on some cold cement floor if he continued in the life. He had come to the mountain top.

Change happened. The first came one night after a walk when he opened the front door and Samantha wasn't there. Nor did she return the next morning, or the next. No note, no phone call; she was gone. He later found two envelopes in his dresser underneath his socks. The outside of one read, "To David from Sam. Educate yourself". When he opened them, stacks of hundred-dollar bills spilled out.

It was the little things that crept along and transformed him, one after the other. His language pattern: the use of "ain't, "shit" and other street words, fell out of his vocabulary. He didn't need to use them. He wore jeans that fit at his waist and not on his hip. He stopped looking to make a score, or to impress some made street king.

Jasmine was dead and that life faded away. When he finally saw his mother, weeks later, she was at home and failing. He cared for her, doing the cooking, laundry, and shopping. He watched her slip away. It also made him grow up. His mother's last wish—it hadn't been easy—came true. The "street" was over, done, but for...this. This damn case.

Fool was no longer ahead of the past he left behind. The court case he fled came a-knocking.

Six Months Later

Chapter Fifty-Four

J.P. sat at the defense table in the courtroom at 26th and California musing at the turn of events over the last six months. He never did call Simone. Instead of talking to her on that day, he went to U. of C. Hospital and met Officer Dietrich in the emergency room—Bay twenty. There were several cops in addition to Dietrich crowded around what he quickly learned was a corpse. The female cop, who went by the name Daniels, cracked jokes, then demanded Dietrich pony up, explaining he'd lost a bet.

Dietrich had a fuck-off grin, ignoring Daniels as best he could, while filling J.P. in on why they were all there, and whether the body was that of Jasmine Taylor.

J.P. took a peek under the sheet. "No, that isn't Jasmine Taylor." Poor Dietrich, another bet lost that he had to pay out.

A voice cut short J.P.'s reminiscences. "Mr. Wilson." The judge had a bemused expression. "Mr. Wilson, are you here? Do you have any questions for this witness?"

J.P. froze. He flashed back to the week after his visit to the U. of C. Hospital. He was served with a summons. Simone had filed a civil suit against him. The bigger surprise happened a few days later. Two detectives showed up at his office.

"We're looking for Josiah Pierson Wilson."

J.P. in his office heard Tasha ask who they were. One of them introduced himself as Detective Bertrand, the other as Detective McCoy.

Tasha didn't have to use the intercom. J.P. came out and saw two burly men. "I'm Mr. Wilson. What's this about?"

"We have an arrest warrant for you."

"A…what?"

"Don't make this more difficult than it has to be," Bertrand said, showing him the paper.

"What's the charge?"

"We'll discuss it at the station. Get your coat."

He had observed this scene a thousand times, but when it happened to him everything seemed to stop. Every sound was distant noise, and people were miles away, even though they were a few feet from him. The mind shut down. He didn't even know he was breathing hard. Seconds that were like hours passed; then survival took over. Things became normal again and so did thinking. Simone—it was her. She had somehow persuaded the cops and State's Attorney to file charges. Jesus H. Christ.

The detective followed him to his office where J.P. grabbed his overcoat. "Detective, I'm not going to give you any trouble. Do you have to cuff me? There's people here."

Bertrand hesitated. "All right, put your hands in front. I'll put your coat over them."

"Thanks."

They walked out of the office. J.P. glanced back at Tasha who was in tears. "It'll be okay," J.P. said, not really believing it himself. "Get hold of Dan Miller."

A gentle shove pushed him out of his office. Twenty-four hours later, after a night in lock-up, he stood before a judge, not as a defense attorney but as the defendant.

"Mr. Wilson," the judge leaned over the bench, "I'm asking if you have any questions of Detective Sanchez?"

"Ah..." J.P. glanced at his yellow legal pad. He hadn't taken a single note during the detective's testimony. His hand had a slight tremor. His stomach felt as if he was on a roller coaster going downhill at a hundred miles per hour. He met the judge's glare, then looked down at the empty page. He could feel his client's, David Lanier, stare going through his store-bought suit jacket. "May I have a moment?" He finally found his voice, his mouth parched. "I would like some water. I seem to have a ..." He began coughing in rapid succession, each cough going deeper as if to exorcise whatever devil was in him.

"There will be a five-minute recess," the judge ordered. "Bailiff, get Mr. Wilson a glass of water." He banged his gavel, then left the bench and disappeared into his chambers.

David's lower jaw dropped. His heart raced, watching Mr. Wilson fall apart, his future getting darker with each of his attorney's retching coughs. He rose from his seat at the defense table and took a few steps to where visitors sat to watch the proceedings. His heart missed a beat as he rubbed his eyes and looked again. Samantha? He hadn't seen her in months. She'd slipped away a week or two after they broke into Big's garage. Jesus. His hand went to his face as seeing her reminded him of the smell of that place.

"You look like you've seen a ghost." Samantha left her seat and met David at the railing dividing the courtroom.

"You're not? You have no problem disappearing. Poof and you're gone." He felt his rage and frustration well into beads of sweat.

She shrugged. "Maybe it's part of my allure."

He wiped his forehead with the back of his hand. Her smile dissipated most of his anger. Still uncomfortable, he shifted his weight from one foot to the other. He took another quick glance at her. "You cut your hair." He knew it sounded dumb. She caught him off-guard. Didn't expect her to be in the courtroom.

"You like it?"

"Yeah, it's good." Like before, a thousand questions filled his mind. *Why did you leave? Where did you go?* Sam…bail. Before he asked a single one, she handed him three long sheets of yellow legal paper.

"I jotted some notes for your lawyer for cross-examination. He's having a rough go at it."

David glanced at the defense table where Mr. Wilson was sipping from his glass. "That's a polite way of looking at the way things are going. Wilson better get it together sooner rather than later or I'm done."

"I believe things will start looking up. Have faith."

He stared at her. "Unbelievable," he said under his breath.

"Give those to J.P." She pointed at the yellow legal papers. "Cheer up, David, nothing is done until it's done."

Chapter Fifty-Five

The bailiff stepped ahead of the judge as he took the bench. "Court is now in session. Remain seated."

David returned to his chair next to his attorney. He held the sheets of paper Samantha handed him and was about to slide them over. "The friend I told you about gave me these," his voice strained. Before Wilson had a chance to look at it the judge interrupted.

"Counsel, are you ready?"

Wilson held up his hand in a gesture for a minute.

"Mr. Wilson, you are trying the court's patience. What is the matter now?"

Wilson took a step away from the defense table. "I mean no disrespect, but my client just passed me several sheets of paper. I'd like to take a minute, your honor."

"One, counsel, that's all you get."

Wilson went through the pages. Gripping them, he leaned over toward David. "Who gave you these?"

"Samantha. She's sitting in the gallery."

They both looked in that direction. "Do you see her?"

David strained studying the faces. He shook his head. "She's gone again."

"Enough. Whatever you're doing with your client needs to stop. Officer Sanchez, please take the stand and remember you are still under oath." The judge leaned back in his chair as Sanchez made his way to the witness chair and Wilson to the defense podium. David could see his lawyer smoothing out Samantha's yellow sheets. Holy Christ, whatever she'd written had to work.

"Officer Sanchez, you arrested my client?"

Damn, we already know he did. David's finger pressed his lips.

"When you arrested him, did you have an arrest warrant?"

The officer shook his head. "No."

"Did you have a search warrant?"

Again, Sanchez said, "No."

"You arrested David Lanier in his house, correct?"

"Counselor, we did not arrest him. We asked him to come with us to the station."

"Ah, and if he refused?"

"We'd take him anyway."

"You handcuffed him?"

Sanchez had a twitch of a smile. "Standard procedure. You should know."

Wilson looked up at the judge. "I'll ask that be stricken."

"It shall. Officer, only answer the question."

Sanchez leaned back in his chair and folded his hands.

"The victim's weapon, money, and jacket you claim my client took, when did you find them?"

Sanchez unfolded his hands. "I'm not sure. I think a week later, maybe two."

"Would it be more accurate to say it was a month afterward?"

"I…I…" Sanchez's gaze went to the prosecutor's table. He looked at the floor. "That may be correct."

Wilson stepped in front of the podium. "I didn't hear you. Please repeat your answer."

Sanchez straightened. His jaw tightened. "That's right, I found the items in the little gangbanger's backyard underneath some pots."

Wilson's voice went up.

"No need," the judge interjected, "your objection to the description of your client is sustained."

Wilson went to his table and snatched several stapled papers. "Please mark this Defendant's Exhibit One for identification and I'm showing them to the prosecution."

"So marked," the judge said.

Wilson faced the witness. "This defendant's One is the search warrant you used to search the defendant's property on the day you found those items. May I approach the witness?"

The judge nodded.

Wilson handed the exhibit to Officer Sanchez.

Sanchez took out his glasses and glanced at the pages, flipping each one when he was done.

"Your search warrant is limited to the house. Isn't that, right?"

Sanchez seemed to flinch, then looked at the search warrant again. "No sir, it says the abode and its contents."

"Is there anything about a backyard and digging up dirt?"

The witness stared straight ahead. After what seemed like a long pause, he said, "No."

"My client was in custody at the time of this search. Correct?"

"I'm not sure."

"He wasn't there when it took place?"

"No."

"There was nothing in the search warrant as well as nothing to indicate that any of the items: the weapon, jacket, and money, would be found outside in the yard in the ground underneath a pot."

Sanchez tilted back. "Are you asking me, counselor?"

"Yeah, yes, I am."

"Well, we were tipped off."

"Great. The warrant, though, was silent as to that tip. Right, Officer Sanchez?"

David leaned forward to catch the witness's answer. It was slow in coming. The judge turned. "Do you understand the question, Officer?"

A heartbeat went by.

"Yes, I do."

"Then answer it."

Sanchez gripped the sides of his chair. "No."

"No, what?"

"The warrant had nothing about searching the backyard or a tip."

"Thank you, Officer. I have no more questions."

Chapter Fifty-Six

"Every time I look at this damn thing, it doesn't get any better." The file labeled the State v. J.P. Wilson rested on Assistant State's Attorney Joclyn Thomas's desk. Various police and lab reports were strewn in front of her and her partner Bob O'Dell as they prepared for the upcoming trial.

Joclyn ran her hand through her hair, then screwed up her face. "We have a month, O'Dell, but I don't think it matters. Time won't make it better. Who the hell approved this piece of shit, anyway?" Joclyn held up the beat officer's report. "Seems to be a bit thin."

"Ours is not to reason why." O'Dell pushed his glasses to the bridge of his nose. "The victim who we are about to prep must have some pull. Aren't we lucky."

"Fuck, after last week, you know we're going to lose the Lanier case. Those cops, Sanchez and his partner, were assholes as well as dirty. The word is they too will soon be indicted. A fuck'n mess. It shouldn't have happened. J.P. ripped them pretty good. They're a lying sack of shit. The judge is going to throw the whole thing out on the Motion to Suppress. You know that."

O'Dell shrugged. "There will always—"

"Then we get this." She took out several more inner files from the main large brown envelope. "Well, the bastard who said yes… and approved this crap… ain't the one who is stuck trying it. It's our reputation that's on the line. The press has been frothing at the mouth and the boss, man oh man."

"It's the city that works."

Joclyn gazed at the ceiling. "For those who have clout."

O'Dell picked up the lab reports, glancing at them. "You know, Joss, there is corroboration to Simone's story. Her clothes were torn. The DNA matched J.P. Her doctor confirmed there was trauma to her vaginal area." He let go of the papers and looked at her. "Were you…how do I say this…eh…"

"Spill it. What are you getting at?"

"Okay. How close were you to J.P.?"

She slapped her desk with her hand, then sprang out of her chair and marched toward their office door. "Are you fucking nuts? The most I can say was we were cordial as professionals. Jesus, O'Dell, just because I'm a woman, I don't have to be a bitch to every male attorney that has business in our courtroom."

"Where are you going?" O'Dell slowly got up. "Sorry Joclyn, but..." he shrugged, "we are in a rumor mill, and I had to ask. To clear the air."

"You cleared it, partner. For the record I never fucked, kissed, or had any relationship with J.P. other than dealing with his cases. If you are so damn interested in J.P.'s affairs, ask Nora." She turned away from O'Dell. "I'm going for coffee. I'll be back in a few minutes." She paused in the doorway. "You know as well as I our alleged victim has cried rape before and the time gap in this case is unexplainable." She didn't want a response; besides, she knew what he'd say. "It's our job. We put it on and let others decide." It's a good excuse for the conscience—gets you out of bed in the morning.

"Your phone is ringing." O'Dell pointed.

"Yeah, it is." She stepped back in and went to her desk and picked up the receiver.

"Your witness is here."

"Thanks, Nora, can you show her to the conference room? We'll be there in a minute."

* * *

Simone stepped out of her shower. She was looking forward to meeting the prosecutors who were going to try her case. The fact that it was going to trial was a win-win for her regardless of the outcome. Whatever testimony comes out in the criminal could be used in the civil where the burden of proof is a mere more likely true than not. So, whatever happens, happens. The damage to J.P.'s reputation would be irreparable.

She checked the time, then opened her walk-in closet. For a girl who started with almost nothing, the amount and quality of her clothes said it all. Suits hung in a row. Another area had dresses, evening gowns, and skirts long and short. There were shelves stacked with sweaters, blouses, and jeans. Some with the tags still hanging.

A towel wrapped around her, she studied each clothing article, discarding some outright, taking others and holding them against her and studying the image in the floor-to-ceiling mirror. She wanted a certain look, one that was not too conservative or liberal. Her gaze fell on a black suit with a beige blouse. Perfect.

She dressed at a leisurely pace, made coffee, and popped a croissant into the microwave. Her appointment with the state's attorneys was for ten o'clock. She'd be late, fashionably so.... by fifteen to twenty minutes. It was always good for control of the situation to build anxiety on the other side. Traffic on the Kennedy was very slow and not knowing she could park in the attorney's lot made finding a space on the street an extended adventure, trying her façade of calmness.

The wind was not a friend as she walked to the office skyscraper attached to the squat courthouse. The day got colder with every step of her two-block walk. She held her coat and purse tightly against her. Gusts of wind assaulted her as she climbed the stairs leading to the entrance. Nearing the top, a long-haired white kid came out from the revolving doors shouting, "free at last, free at last," then ran past wearing a short sleeve shirt and jeans still yelling and praising Jesus. A few of her fellow entrants stopped to look, most of the others ignored him and moved as quickly as they could to get inside. A sheriff greeted her once she got through the door, barking instructions.

"Your purses and everything in your pockets goes on the conveyer along with your coat." She tried to ask for directions to the state's attorney's office, but he would have none of it. He pointed to the machine. "Got to keep the line moving, lady."

Her purse set off the sensors. "Step out," a female sheriff ordered. The woman's nametag read Crosby. She opened Simone's purse and rummaged through it without asking permission, holding up a gold case. "What's this?"

Simone was panicked as well as embarrassed. "Birth control." She kept her voice down.

"Birth control in this?" The sheriff didn't wait for a response but opened the container. "Looks to me that be something else. Since when do birth control come in powder form?"

"Look, I have an appointment with the state's attorney's office." She looked at her watch. "I'm late."

"Honey, it looks like you may have more problems than you already have. What is this stuff, 'cause you know what it looks like."

"It isn't that. I don't use drugs...not that kind anyway. What you're holding is...is a performance enhancer. You mix a small portion in water. It gives a boost."

"Uh-huh."

"It's concentrated bovine."

"Say what?"

"Really, you can buy it at any of those specialty health stores...also Amazon." Shit, she heard herself speaking fast. Her nerves were showing.

"Wait here. You better not move." Crosby used her radio to contact her captain.

"Officer, I'm not kidding. I'm to meet with Joclyn Thomas and Robert O'Dell, and I'm late, very late."

"Nothing I can do about it until the captain looks at this stuff. If you give me any more lip, I'll handcuff you and take you into custody. Your choice."

Simone wasn't going to be bullied. She had another card to play. "Can I use my phone? I'd like to call Sheriff Thompson. He's a personal friend. I have his private cell number. If you give me my phone...."

"You know the *Cook County Sheriff*?"

Simone straightened. "He's a friend of mine. Went to Penn State... in theater together. Romeo and Juliet. Guess who he played."

"Ma'am, I don't want to hear no more." Crosby went into Simone's purse and dug out her cell. "Let's see."

"No problem." Simone went to her contacts and there it was. "Should I call?"

Crosby looked around and not hearing or seeing the captain, returned Simone's purse as well as the gold case. "Twelfth floor. Take the elevator by the small concession stand."

Simone grabbed her things and walked toward the elevators. She checked her watch. Fashionably late wasn't late at all.

Chapter Fifty-Seven

David and his lawyer said little in the elevator that took them to the main floor of the courthouse. He wondered what was going on in his attorney's mind. *Jesus, how the mighty has fallen; all that coughing and taking no notes. Thank God for Samantha, wherever she is. Where did all his fine suits go?* He could tell the material looked store-bought and certainly not custom. David had to hand it to him though, with all the crap about Mr. Wilson's upcoming criminal trial, he came through. As they neared the exit, David broke the silence. "What do you think?"

Wilson stopped. He seemed to consider it for a moment. "It was a good day. The judge should suppress everything found at your house."

"That's great." David stopped before going through the revolving doors. "You said should…"

"If there's one thing I've learned, David, it's never over until it is. All I can tell you it looks good."

David gave it a minute to digest. "Nothing else to do but to take it. Better than a kick in the pants."

Wilson nodded. "Don't forget the next court date. See ya."

David went out the door. Fierce wind blew through his thin coat as he went down the stairs. *Jesus it's damn cold.* He still didn't own a car and was debating whether to take the bus or an Uber. He reached the sidewalk, and his eye went to a chocolate-colored Mercedes convertible that was idling. As he neared, the passenger window went down.

"Get in, David."

"Samantha?"

He opened the front passenger door and climbed in. "What the fu…"

"Ssh. You have every right to be pissed, confused, angry, and whatever other negative feelings you have. Have a bit more patience and some, if not all of it, will be explained."

She pulled away from the curb.

"At least tell me where we're going?"

"Better to wait. You like it?"

He touched the soft leather of the dash as well as the seat. "What happened to the Beamer?"

She made a face, then shrugged.

"It's another one of Sam's vanishing cars?"

"Sort of, but this one is mine. Sam had nothing to do with it."

"Really?"

"Most of it, anyway. I paid. He negotiated."

"Sam? He's around? I haven't heard from him since…" He touched his chin, "since Indiana, or, I think it was Indiana."

Samantha gave him a quick glance.

"What aren't you saying?"

"You're like the kid waiting for Santa. Really, David."

He swallowed all of his questions. She wouldn't answer anyway. He'd keep it light, the weather…the…weather…oh hell…. "Thanks for helping out today. Whatever you wrote got Wilson going. You should have seen him."

"Great. The cop was lying his ass off."

"You saw?"

"Not the cross, but when he testified on direct."

"Hold on where…how…I mean…where's this legal language coming from?"

She changed lanes, heading for the Dan Ryan Expressway North.

"Why did you do that?

"To get on the Kennedy. We're going to Lincolnwood."

"Lincolnwood? Why?"

She shook her index finger. "I told you…" She winked. "Pizza."

"Should I believe that?"

"Up to you."

"Okay. I love surprises." He looked away and stared at the passing scenery.

Chapter Fifty-Eight

Simone brushed her hair back waiting for the elevator to take her to the twelfth floor. She glared at the floor indicator and couldn't believe that after several minutes the damn thing hadn't moved. *What else could go wrong?* A crowd was beginning to form.

Simone turned to a young man dressed in a suit. "Is this usual?"

"Oh, yeah. Hopefully it doesn't get stuck. The other day it didn't make it beyond five. If you're here for jury duty take the elevator behind me."

"No, I'm to see Joclyn Thomas on twelve."

"Oh," and slowly looked away.

What the hell does that mean? She drew her purse closer and stared at the red flashing light now signaling the car was on two. The crush of people drew closer in anticipation.

Simone was still recovering from the close call she had with the sheriff... thank God for Crosby's boss, Sheriff Thompson. The occasional small favors paid off. She even sort of liked the guy, but business was business. She needed to be more careful, though. There's always a price to pay for dumb mistakes.

A small bell sound announced the elevator's arrival. Those trying to get out fought their way through the incoming throng. No wonder why these things get stuck. A cart full of files nudged her to the back of the car. The driver of it said a terse apology, then shouted to someone toward the front, "Push twelve." Jesus.

For the amount of people stuffed in the car, there was a plume of quiet except for the "excuse me" when persons fought their way out as they reached their destination. The elevator did its best to scare the crap out of its inhabitants, creaking and lurching its way upward. By the twelfth floor, there was only Simone, a file cart, and the person she met at the beginning of the journey. When the door slid open, he pointed Simone to reception.

"Thank you." She went to her left and he to her right. It was only a few steps before she opened the glass door with State's Attorney's Office stenciled in large black letters.

"Can I help you?" the young woman seated at the desk inquired. Her name plate read Nora James.

Before Simone could answer, she said, "You must be Ms. Jenwick. I'll let the attorneys know." She picked up the phone and after a short conversation, told Simone to follow her to a conference room. There was something about the way this Nora James looked at her that didn't feel right.

"Have we met?"

Nora shook her head. "I don't think so, unless you've hung around here."

"No, first time in this building."

"I'm sure you'd remember the experience. I did when I started several years ago."

They walked down a hallway until Nora stopped and opened a door to a glass-enclosed room. "Have a seat. The attorneys should be here in a few minutes."

Simone could feel Nora's eyes on her. "You sure we haven't…"

"No, I'm sure. There's water if you need it in the corner." Nora let the door close behind her.

Simone took a seat in the middle of the conference table. She fought the urge to look at her phone, and finally gave in. She was reviewing her emails when the attorneys walked in carrying a thick file.

"Good morning," Joclyn said, introducing herself and her partner. She didn't waste time with any more pleasantries but launched into a brief summation of the do's and don'ts in testifying. "The key is to only answer the question asked. Do not add things or most importantly…guess."

Simone nodded. "I know. Unfortunately, I've done this before."

Joclyn cleared her throat before responding. "Good, then you know the rules."

"I do. Would you like me to go through my testimony?"

Joclyn quickly glanced at O'Dell. "In a minute. First, I'd like you to look at the defense's witness list that was emailed to us a day ago. I'm not concerned with the police; it's the other names."

She slid the paper across the table. Simone opened her purse and rummaged for her glasses. The first thing she felt was the gold case. *Shit.*

She looked up, a tight smile on her face, then plunged her hand deeper. "I need them only for reading." She could feel her cheeks redden. "They're a pain. I waste so much time trying to find them." Her hand finally clutched the form of a cloth case. "Ah, here they are." She held it up. "Sorry for the delay." She snapped the button of the holder and put them on. "I can see." She gave a small laugh. She picked up the paper and read, running her finger down the list of names. She came to the last and dropped the sheet.

"Any surprises?"

Simone glanced at the paper again. "No…I don't…" She used her finger, again reviewing the names until she got to the last one. She picked the document up and held it closer to her. "Who's he?" She pointed.

Joclyn leaned forward. "Robert Lanier. You don't know?"

Chapter Fifty-Nine

J.P. sighed as he watched David leave the building. He should have felt great. Victory was in their grasp, but the turmoil in his stomach didn't allow for celebration.

In the last six months, he must have aged a decade. The cost of defending the civil and criminal lawsuits against him was painful. Gone was his purchase of custom-made clothing. He downsized his vehicle to an everyman Honda Accord. His glittering big office was no more. It was him and Tasha. The news coverage haunted him everywhere and new clients shied away. He was no longer the "golden boy." His wings were tarnished and if it wasn't for those notes David gave him…the case would have been lost. What occurred in the courtroom…his mind going adrift had been happening too frequently.

Simone had crawled into his head and taken up residence. Whenever there was a lull anywhere or anyplace, a court's proceedings, driving… he'd play back the scene of that night and beat himself for not being more aware of the danger signs. "Tear my clothes," she said, her voice ringing in his ear. Why didn't he stop? He knew the answer to that one. All men knew the answer. The dick had a power and momentum of its own. Then again, why? Should he have given in and made that telephone call? *What's a few bucks compared to the misery Simone has caused?* The questions were never resolved. They fired in his mind, one after the other.

The buzz of his cell phone interrupted his musings. He retrieved it from his pocket. It took him several seconds to recognize the number was his attorney, Dan Miller.

"Hey Dan, what's up?

"Where are you, J.P.?"

"Twenty-sixth Street, why?"

"Can you come by this afternoon. I have something to show you."

"Sure, has Simone given up?"

There was a pause. "No, but…I'll see you soon."

J.P. returned the phone to his pocket. *What was that about?* He took a breath. He had made like announcements either in person or on the phone a thousand times to his clients. For some, it brought good news, smiles on faces and a win in his book. Others, it was like a doctor delivering a bad diagnosis. J.P. watched, not letting his emotions show, as the client's face became sullen or serious, and a whispered "Thanks" escaped their lips with, "We'll let you know what we decide."

Miller's call set J.P.'s mind wondering. Did he hear hope in Miller's voice or the end of the road for him? He half wanted to go to Gene's, a bar down the block, kick back with a beer, and mull it over, but life had a rhythm, unique to each and the current didn't allow for that luxury.

He drew himself up and prayed there was no one from the press hanging around outside the front of the courthouse. He eyed the time on his watch. It was late enough that it was possible. Gone were the days when attorneys as well as court visitors would stop him for a greeting or a few words.

Simone had succeeded in making him a pariah, a contemptible sex fiend who should rot in hell. He had to admit, he'd underestimated her ability to use social media. She was very good at it.

He went through the revolving doors, ignoring the ever-present wind, and walked head down, navigating the stairs in quick strides. The parking lot was across the small park and the boulevard. Like a football player evading tacklers, he moved quickly through the grounds until he was stopped before crossing the street by a large Black man with a two-day old beard. The garage driveway was on the other side.

"Hey, brother, you a lawyer?"

This was not a conversation J.P. wanted. He nodded, while trying to sidestep the stranger.

"Hey man, I'm talk'n to you. You have a ten spot? I'll pay you tomorrow. I have a sick kid."

J.P. had been around long enough to believe the man was lying. Despite that, what if he wasn't? What if this guy was undercover, or Simone had something to do with it. Jesus. Or what if he was who he appeared to be, a Black man down on his luck. He had to admire the man's chutzpah, asking for ten dollars and not a buck. Even begging had been inflated.

He stole another glance… tattered coat, worn shoes. Was he looking at himself? Could this be him in the future? J.P. took a breath. No sir, no way. It wasn't going to happen, Simone be damned. Ten bucks wasn't going to make any difference in J.P.'s life despite his legal troubles. He fished around in his pants pocket and pulled out a five and a one. "It's all I have. Hope your kid is better." J.P. stuffed the bills in the man's hand and crossed the street without looking back.

* * *

Dan Miller's office was across the Chicago River in one of the newer towers that had sprung up like beanstalks at the end of the 1990's. J.P. found parking on Clark Street a few blocks distant. He didn't mind the walk but for the ever-present wind. Once inside the building, he presented himself to reception/security and received his visitor's pass. Unlike 26th and California complex, the elevator whisked him to Miller's office on the fortieth floor with no trouble. He stepped out and walked the few feet to his attorney's door. He grasped the handle and took a deep breath. Like J.P.'s many clients before, he wondered if this would be a hallelujah moment or more misery. He looked upward for a second, then entered the outer office.

The woman at the reception desk looked up and didn't bother with a greeting. "Mr. Wilson, Dan is waiting for you. I'll let him know you've arrived."

"Thanks." J.P. took a seat. He glanced at one of the newspapers on the table, thought about the *Wall Street Journal* lying next to it, then decided not to look at any. Instead, he folded his hands and waited.

Dan came out from the interior and stuck his hand out. "Hey, J.P., good to see you. Come on in."

They shook hands and J.P. followed into his office. It was all glass.

"You ever walk into that?" J.P. pointed to the door.

"Me? I must admit it had happened once or twice." He shrugged. "My partners wanted an airy look. They weren't concerned about privacy. I was outvoted."

"If the sun cooperated, you'd have to wear sunglasses all day. A hell of a view, though."

Dan glanced toward the windows. "Yeah." He turned to J.P. "They're tinted. So, you don't have to."

J.P. nodded. "The architects did their job." He sat back, taking in the file on Dan's desk which, if he were to guess, was about him. His fingers did a little tap on the armrest. *Who cares about the construction of the damn office?*

"I called you," Dan broke the tension, "because I think I have some good news…very good news. I was in the process of preparing our witness list when I received a voice mail left on my cell. A person wanted to talk to me about your matter. We met this morning. You were in court, otherwise I would have had you come in. We're in the process of checking the story out. Should have all that we need by tomorrow, then I'm adding the name to our list and sending it to the state."

J.P.'s heart pounded so fast. He thought it might burst. J.P. wiped his face with his hand and shook his head. "That's great…that's great…good news," he said over and over. He looked at Dan. His eyes misted. "Jesus, I ain't too emotional, am I. So much for professionalism." He grabbed a tissue from a box on the side table. "Sorry, I'm usually on your side of the desk."

Dan nodded and grinned. "I think this person's testimony will blow…no pun intended, Simone out of the water."

"Who is it? Can you tell me?"

"Sure. Do you know a Robert Lanier?"

Chapter Sixty

"I know I'm not to ask questions, but come on, Samantha, what are we doing here? This sure doesn't look like the pizza place—"

Her wide smile cut him off. "You'll see."

They had parked in Beth Shalom's parking lot. "We're in a temple's parking lot."

"I know. Get out of the car."

He unhooked his seat belt and followed her to the side door of the building. "I haven't been in one of these since…well, right before my Bar Mitzvah that didn't happen. What the hell are you doing?"

She laughed.

"You look so happy torturing me." He touched her arm. "Really, Samantha why are we here?"

"I want you to meet someone."

"Why all the mystery?"

Her eyes sparkled. "The person is very mysterious."

She pressed the buzzer and seconds later, the door opened. They walked down a corridor into an office area.

"Hello, Samantha," an older woman called from her desk. A button on her landline was blinking. She glanced at it. "He's in there," pointing to an office with the door shut. "He's on the phone yelling up a storm. I bet he's bawling out one of the caterers. Never a dull moment." She shifted slightly toward her desk computer. "And who is this?" Looking at David.

"Let me introduce you. David this is Lill, the best damn secretary, office manager, and caretaker of everything and everybody."

"You're too kind, but it's true. If I left for an hour, the putz," she pointed to the office door, then shrugged, "sorry, Samantha…"

"It's okay and probably true."

"Go on in. It'll do him good to be interrupted. Don't bother knocking. He won't hear you…too busy jabbering."

"Okay."

They could hear his raised voice as Samantha opened the door. David for a moment wasn't sure or believed, but after listening to several more rapid sentences...recognition. "Sam? Is that you?"

The person sitting behind a large desk had his back to the door and the phone cord over his shoulder.

"Sam?" David said it louder.

Samantha went over and tapped the man on his shoulder. "Dad, David is here."

"Dad? Did you just call him..."

"Yes, the person you know as Sam is my father. You better sit down."

"Got to go," Sam swiveled in his chair and hung up the phone. "Boychik, how have you been? You look a bit pale. Samantha, get him something to drink."

David found a seat in one of the overstuffed chairs in front of the desk. "That's okay, I don't need anything." The questions he kept locked down came welling up, but he didn't say anything. His lips trembled, but no words came. He couldn't sit. He stood, walked around the room, then leaned on the chair.

"Sit, David. Hear me out and hopefully your questions will be answered. Samantha, get him some water, please." Sam took out a handkerchief and dabbed his forehead.

David sat deep in the chair. His hands covered his face.

"Before..." Sam glanced at the bookcase by the wall and began again. "First, I am your father's brother. Sol and I didn't get along much and especially around the time of your bar mitzvah and his death. I was at your parents' wedding but after that...that's probably why you didn't know of me."

David dropped his hands. "What?"

"I'll try to be gentle but there is no nice way of saying what I'm about to tell you." He loosened his tie and cleared his throat. "Your father had an affair with a woman. Unbeknownst to me, I was also seeing the same lady. When I found out...well...your father didn't take it well. He thought I told your mother. I hinted it to her... a call out of the blue. Don't know how she took it." Sam took a deep breath. "I had no idea it would lead to his death, but it did."

"Hold on, hold on. My dad was fooling around on my old lady?" He shook his head. "Wow...hard to believe. This is too much." He twisted open the water bottle Samantha had brought and took a drink. "And you're my uncle?" David was half on and half off the chair. "That would make Samantha my…my cousin…holy crap…first cousin."

Sam nodded. "There's more."

"Holy shit. More?"

"Buckle up." He stepped from his desk and stood next to another chair across from David. Samantha came alongside him. "This woman who we were both seeing vanished after your father died only to re-emerge a month or two later. She called me, never apologizing but then told me she was pregnant. She believed the father was either me or Sol. She went on to say that years ago she had a daughter and Sol was the father. Anne of course did not know. As long as Sol was alive, she agreed to raise that child. Now that Sol was dead, things changed. She made me an offer which at the time I resented but…" he touched Samantha's arm, "I'm very glad I took. She was going to blackmail Anne, your mother and me, if I didn't accept. Of course I did. As to the pregnancy, she claimed, I don't know what happened. Once I agreed I didn't hear from her again."

"She did that?" Samantha took a step away from her father. "Huh." She brushed her hair from her face.

David got up and paced. "This isn't happening." He stared at them, then pointed. "So, you…Samantha…could be…could…," his voice trailed off, "my half-sister? Holy fuck…oh shit…excuse…Jesus…" He slumped back in his chair. "You knew?" He stared at Samantha, then waved his hand. "Of course you did. That sort of explains why…why you left. Poof."

"It was for the best, David."

"If you say so." He folded his hands against his chest and rocked. "I could have used… I… on my God. What if…?"

"I know, but I did it for the both of us. This day would come sooner or later, and we'd regret it. Dad warned me not to get involved but I did anyway. He was right in one sense but I'm so glad we met. Hey, I got a brother out of it and unlike a lover, ours is forever."

"One way to put it." He scratched the side of his head. "This is like one of them Netflix series. Now what? I've gone from no family to an uncle, a sister, and a past which I didn't know. Wow, wow." He gulped more water.

"If I thought of my old man at all I never saw him like that. My mom did everything, tried to anyway. She kept me going. Watching her bravery in her last month gave me the courage to change. I don't know…like wow. Sam, uncle…my uncle. Jesus." He glanced at the ceiling. "Oops, shouldn't have said that in here." He stood next to a photo of Jerusalem that hung on the wall. "What a day. I can't…" He stretched to his full height. "How things change." He let that sink in for a moment. "My past has been wiped clean. The stuff I didn't understand or didn't want to; about me, my mom, my dad. Jesus. Why the street seemed better than my home." A shiver went through him. "Hey, you know, Mr. Wilson feels good about my case. All of this could be behind me. I could be free."

Sam put his hand on his nephew's shoulder. "It's no longer you against the world. It never was."

Chapter Sixty-One

Simone felt Joclyn eyeing her. There was no doubt the bitch wanted to catch her in a misstatement or out-and-out lie. *Jesus, who's on trial here?*

"You don't know who Robert Lanier is?"

Simone studied the paper again, then shrugged, "No. Should I?"

Joclyn leaned over the table and grabbed the sheet. "Why would he be on the defendant's witness list if you don't know him? He's not mentioned in any police reports, lab, or supplementals."

"You make it sound like I'm hiding something."

"Are you?"

"Of course not. That would be stupid, don't you think? I want J.P. put away. He's a danger to women, not just me." She glanced at O'Dell. "To all of us. Shouldn't we be concentrating on that? You do have investigators. Go find out."

Joclyn cleared her throat. "We'll take care of it. Let's go through your witness preparation."

Simone spent the next forty-five minutes going over her testimony. She had practiced at home to know when to pause, when to shed a tear, and when to answer in a shaky voice. "This is very difficult for me. Every time I retell it, I have nightmares. J.P. ruined me. I can't…I mean…how do you trust…" She looked at O'Dell. "I don't mean to offend you. I'd like to believe not all men are like… but I hope you understand."

O'Dell nodded. "No offense taken. You've held up well. As the trial date gets closer, we'll revisit it again. Thank you for coming."

Simone shook each attorney's hand. They then walked her to the elevator. As Simone stepped into the car, she turned to face them. "If you find this Robert Lanier, let me know."

"Sure will," Joclyn said as the elevator door closed.

The ride down was much smoother than the ride up. She reached the main floor and left the building. On her way out, she made sure she didn't run into Sheriff Croft, Crosby or whatever her name was —once was more than enough. *What an almost fiasco. Thank God for clout.*

The walk to her car made her realize, though, it would be only a matter of time before she heard from the Sheriff himself. That's how things worked. She shrugged; everything has a price. She got in her vehicle and slammed the door. Once on the road, she shifted to the more important issue… Robert Lanier. She told that bitch of a state's attorney the truth. She didn't know Robert Lanier. She knew him as Sam. Robert was his middle name.

Chapter Sixty-Two

Simone arrived home, went to the family room, and lit the logs in the fireplace. It took no time at all, especially since it was gas. She poured herself a scotch, nothing fancy but one that fit the day. It had been years since she'd visited her diary that was kept locked in her safe behind the bookshelf. It was time. She should have gotten rid of it, years ago, but call her sentimental. She retrieved it and settled in her easy plush chair with drink in hand. "Sam! Gawd," and opened the book.

Sam was the fun one. Sol may have been romantic at first, then affairs as they often do become complicated. I became pregnant a few years after Anne. Sol knew. How Anne didn't find out then was a testament to secrets well kept. Or Anne's typical way of not seeing what was obvious. Between Sol's lack of nerve and the demands of a newborn, I grew restless.

Simone looked up and gritted her teeth.

Motherhood was nice, but that wasn't what I had planned for myself. My daughter had a string of nannies and babysitters. Life was too damn short to be confined to mothering. Baby talk led nowhere.

She glanced away from the yellowed pages and took a deep breath. She told herself this was not the occasion for remorse and read on.

I met Sam at a charity auction. I had begun to work at a merchandise jobbing company and near the holidays their bank threw a party where the proceeds went to good causes. Sam ran the auction. The man was smooth and could sell ice to an Eskimo. He won me over in a New York minute. He introduced himself as Sam but later, that night in the luxury of my bed, told me he used his middle name, Robert, in business dealings.

Simone ran a hand down her side to her hip.

Where Sol was slow and methodical, Sam grabbed what he wanted and made me feel good doing it. Having the both of them, separately of course, was a class in eroticism. It was also a balancing act that eventually came crashing down.

Simone decided she needed a cube of ice for her drink. She went downstairs, retrieved one and plopped it in her glass. She liked the sound of the clink as she made her way back. She settled in her chair, glancing at the dancing flames of the fire, and steeled herself.

It was a night where I didn't plan better. Too many things going on.

"Oh yeah…lots of everything."

My daughter was no longer a baby and demanded more care. I was rising in my company and there was more responsibility and challenges. It took a lot of energy to balance life. It was a January evening, and I failed. I met Sol for dinner and then we went back to a second apartment I and Sol rented. We had wine, more than I should have. I forgot I had arranged for Sam to come for pizza. It was an ugly scene.

She sat up.

Sam came in the front as the back door closed. The bedroom was unmade, and Sam found a credit card with Sol's name. Of course I wasn't wearing much, either. My lying skills weren't adept and sharp. Sam had no problem figuring it out.

Simone took a long swallow of the scotch. She felt the burn in the back of her throat and coughed. Another sip, thinking while she fingered the rim of the glass. She closed the diary and let it fall to the floor. She could recite her very thoughts and half shut her eyes.

She had to find a way out of her predicament. She asked, but perhaps it was a demand, for Sol to leave his wife. Sol's response was to hang himself. The poor man never reconciled love for her and the guilt that made him stay with Anne. This was too much. She left town and took a month or two to figure out what to do. After she realized she was pregnant again, there was no longer the luxury of time. She wouldn't have another kid, and the one she had needed a better home. It was all for the best. Sam saw it that way, too, after a little persuasion. He realized the stench of an affair with him was not the kind of thing that earns promotions, especially in the banking and finance field. As for Anne, that knowledge would also affect her business. Better to stay quiet. Sol was dead. It was best for everyone.

Simone tapped her glass. There was a little left of the liquid and she gulped it down. What to do? If Sam got on the stand, his testimony would ruin her. No jury or judge would have much sympathy for her. No, Sam would not only destroy her cases against J.P., but she could be financially ruined as well. He was indeed a threat, and threats must be dealt with one way or another.

How ironic life was. After she gave up her daughter, Sam and Samantha disappeared. Never heard from either. She put the glass down on the little side table and rubbed her hands, her vision blurred by the flames. The remains of ash evidence of the logs it had once been. The crack of the dissolved ice broke the fire's mesmerizing power. She turned, glanced at her empty glass, then got up. In the bathroom she splashed cold water on her face and after drying, looked into the mirror. She didn't blink. Her face and body had held up well despite passing years. She had wealth, a place in society. She had made the climb. But out of nowhere a tear trickled down. The past was really never past despite the distance travelled.

Chapter Sixty-Three

David walked through the door held by the doorman and into a restaurant called Steak 48 on Wabash. It took a minute or two to adjust to the darkness and the hum of a place that was jumping. The people, from what he could finally see, were dressed to the nines: tailored clothing on fit bodies.

When he'd received the invitation from Samantha, she didn't tell him the dress code. He figured if Sam had anything to do with it, he ought to do better than jeans. A tie was a step too far. He weighed whether it was a good idea, though. His clothing selections were limited, and he wasn't all that comfortable in fancy restaurants, despite Sam's previous attempts. The thought of going back to court the next day also weighed on him. What if the judge doesn't suppress the evidence? What if…he went back and forth and finally decided to go. He chose a sweater look and a decent pair of slacks.

"Excuse me, I'm here with the Sam Lanier party?" He had to raise his voice to be heard. The hostess took his breath away. Tall and willowy with dark hair flowing to her shoulders, she poked her iPad, then smiled. "Sam and his guests are already here. Patrick will show you the way."

David wound his way carefully not to bump into any tables or people. They walked around the open kitchen area until Patrick stopped and pointed to an all-glass enclosure. "Enjoy your dinner."

Sam and Samantha were seated across the table from Mr. Wilson. "Sit, boychik, Samantha told me you weren't sure, I'm glad you decided to come celebrate."

David sat, adjusting the glass and silverware on the table. "My court date is tomorrow. Isn't this a little early?"

Sam brushed the air with his hand. "Don't worry, J.P. thinks you're a winner." He winked.

"Glad he told you."

"In my defense, David, that isn't exactly what I said but…"

"Besides, we're not only celebrating you, David, but J.P. too. After I testify in his matter, which, I believe is in two weeks, justice will be done." Sam raised his glass. "Let's drink to that."

"Hear hear." They all lifted their Champagne glasses already filled on the table.

"Now, I don't want any arguments, this dinner is on me. Have whatever you want."

David checked the menu, and his eyes widened. "Are you going to get a bank loan to pay for this? Holy..."

"I'm in the business. Wouldn't be a problem."

Everyone laughed.

"I've been blessed not just my success..."

"He owns half the city," Samantha blurted. "I mean with financing real estate, restaurants, cars, you name it."

"Thanks, dear, what I was going to say, besides the financial, more important are you and now David my blessings."

"Aww, thanks, Dad."

The first of many courses arrived. At the end of the meal, after the dessert, a shot of Macallan's 18 for J.P., and many thanks, they got up to leave.

Sam tapped David's shoulder. "Would you mind walking me to my apartment? It's not far. There's something I want to discuss."

* * *

Simone didn't wait for the State or its investigators to find Robert Lanier. The business world through her own contacts and LinkedIn was just as chatty as any gossip column. She learned he had several places: a condo in River North, a home in Lincolnwood, and other properties in Indiana, California, and Arizona. Sam had done well, as she thought he would.

She had about two weeks. There wasn't time for an elaborate scheme. He most likely wouldn't be persuaded by money. Given his lifestyle, he probably had more than enough. Sex—always a possibility, but not probable. That left only two things...persuasion, the threat she had used before: or elimination. She also learned he spent Sundays and Mondays at his condo. Her plan came into focus. She'd pay him a visit.

Thank God for doormen who appreciated a skintight little black dress and had a fondness for Grants and Franklins. The doorman told her Sam had left for dinner but would be back later that evening. She told the dear she was a surprise, kind of like a gift for something nice Sam had done. His facial expression didn't change as he discreetly stuffed one bill after another in his pocket and let her into Sam's apartment.

Sam had a hell of a place. It looked north and east from the 51st floor. The living room was sheer glass. She took a step toward it. One could see the lake and Lake Shore Drive—a splendid view. Her heels clicked on the parquet floor. Set on a table was a glass vase that looked like it was a Chihuly. "Tsk, tsk, the man has expensive and good taste." Farther into the apartment were two bedrooms, an exercise room, an office, three bathrooms, and the master bedroom full of paintings, doors with gold trim with a view of the city looking north. *Damn him.*

She returned to the living room and picked out a high-backed chair facing the spectacular sights to wait.

Darkness settled over the city and low-intensity lights turned on in the apartment. In some ways, it was like an out-of-body experience to be in Sam's place, after all these years. Things, she supposed, could have been different if, instead of having Sol, she had met Sam first, but one doesn't always get to choose. She was in her twenties, too young and stupid. She convinced herself Sol wanted passion, love, and he'd leave Anne. As the old saying goes, "man plans, and God laughs." *Here we are.*

She heard the thrust of a key and click of the lock. Her body tensed. Her senses stretched to the extreme. She listened to the footsteps in the hallway. There was someone with Sam, as she heard two voices. Shit. No bargaining now, no conversation. It's either him or her. Whoever was with him, was unfortunately wrong place, wrong time. She reached into her oversized bag for her Smith and Wesson and pointed to the space where the edge of the hallway met the living room. She saw the shadows of two figures approach, their voices louder, clearer. She fired. The explosions of several shots rang in her ear.

Seconds later, someone returned fire.

Chapter Sixty-Four

The bailiff in the courtroom hit the side of the bench with his hand. "Please rise, this court is in session. The Honorable Judge Edmonds presiding. Please be seated."

J.P. was dressed in his best blue suit. He kept looking for David. He had called him, but there was no answer. He reached out to Samantha, but she hadn't responded.

The Judge looked to his right. "I notice the State's attorneys have not…"

The courtroom door flew opened and Joclyn stepped in, followed by O'Dell who pushed the file cart. "Sorry your honor, but we were delayed by a call regarding a case, or I should say cases." She glanced at J.P. "Would the clerk first call the State v. David Lanier."

J.P. rose from his seat and mouthed, "What is going on?"

Joclyn had reached the State's podium. "Your honor, we have," she took a breath, "received information the defendant in this matter, David Lanier, is deceased. Therefore, the state makes a motion of cause abated death suggested."

"What?"

Joclyn held up her hand. "Further, Judge, the state has motioned up the matter of State v. J.P. Wilson, and although this is a bit unusual, we will make a motion to dismiss as our witness, Simone Jenwick, is deceased. We have notified Mr. Wilson's attorney, Dan Miller, of our intention, and he has agreed to allow us to proceed."

J.P. had a hand by his heart and sat down.

"Do you wish to object, counsel?"

J.P. could only shake his head.

"Counsel you must verbally respond."

Somehow, he found his voice, "No objection."

"That being the case, these matters are dismissed."

* * *

It ain't cool being dead.

Fool never liked funerals. Too much bawl'n and dudes come'n up say'n they're sorry and all that shit. His old lady took it hard. Her hand on his shoulder lean'n on him. She perk'd up see'n a dude who was hang'n back—like he didn't want to be seen but not totally. He sort of had my old man's looks but a hell of lot better. He didn't come forward or say noth'n, but my old lady mouthed somethin' and then he was gone. Never did find out who that was.

* * *

Sam wiped his forehead with his sleeve as he sat in his wheelchair, his leg bandaged, near David's soon-to-be grave. Samantha was next to him dressed in black but chic. Instead of overcast and ugly, the skies were clear, and the sun bright. Mr. Wilson and Nora were also there sitting graveside.

The rabbi from Beth Shalom, must have been Sam's doing, spoke a few words, said all the right things, then Mr. Wilson took a turn.

He stood with his back to the hole in the ground that would be David's final resting place. His black yarmulke sat uncomfortably on his head. He wore the same blue suit he wore in court the other day. His voice was steady, rich in its tenor. He wasn't called a great mouthpiece for nothing. He moved away from the microphone. He didn't need it and began. "Sam was David's guardian angel, if there is such a thing. He was there at David's father's funeral, and he kept tabs on David… unseen but there. Sam made it his obligation, and he succeeded. He saw to it David got on the right track. He didn't force him but provided the light and the means.

"That night in Sam's apartment, his protective shield collapsed. After the first shots, as he fell, it was David who returned fire. Was it luck or God's will David was with Sam that evening? We don't know. We will never know. Those are mysteries left to others to explain. The fact that David had a weapon with him, is telling."

Mr. Wilson took a handkerchief from his front pocket and wiped his face. He took a deep breath, then rocked on his heels and continued. "The street is a hard place to grow up. I've seen it and lived it. The street is tough and unyielding. David learned well. It taught him how to survive. Packing a weapon was as natural as putting on shoes. The street made you see things that many, not accustomed to its ways, miss. David understood the demands. As he always said, 'You got to stay ahead of what's behind.'"

Also by Jerome G. Silbert

Hide & Seek

Nicole was at the top of her game. Now she was dead.

She was moving up in the corporate world fast, applying her brains and charms to those who helped her climb. There was Jim, her co-worker; Charlie, a cop; J.K., her boss and the Chairman of the Board; Mr. Hill, J.K.'s man for all seasons; and, of course, Neve, J.K.'s daughter. Nicole had it all until it ended one night. The Medical Examiner wrote the cause of her death as "Undetermined."

To Detectives Brandt and his partner, Charlie Young, something about Nicole's death felt amiss. It didn't make sense why Nicole, so successful, should die so unexpectedly. Young, who knew Nicole all too well, never told anyone about their relationship. Love and sex held many secrets.

Yet, despite her many successes—or maybe because of them—everyone had a motive for doing away with Nicole. For some, it was a betrayal of their trust and love. For others, it was Nicole's potential use of power and confidence.

Was the truth of Nicole's death hidden in plain sight? Soon, the suspect tagged as "it" would reveal the "who" in life's real game of hide and seek.

Available from all major book dealers.

www.ingramcontent.com/pod-product-compliance
Lightning Source LLC
LaVergne TN
LVHW100308210926
848480LV00003B/1058